P9-AQV-592

Favorite Psalms

Growing Closer to God

Selected and expounded by
John Stott

Rector Emeritus,
All Souls Church, Langham Place, London

Presented at the First
Charles Simeon Sermons
November 9-12, 2004

Dr. John R. W. Stott,
Inaugural Expositor

TAYLOR
UNIVERSITY

BAKER
A DIVISION OF
Baker Book House Co

Copyright © 1988, 2003 by John R. W. Stott

Published by Baker Books
a division of Baker Book House Company
P.O. Box 6287
Grand Rapids, MI 49516–6287

First printing, 2003

ISBN 0 8010 6472 4

All rights reserved.
No part of this publication may be reproduced,
or transmitted in any form or by any means,
electronic or mechanical, including photocopy,
recording, or any information storage and retrieval system,
without permission in writing from the publisher.

Scripture quotations in this publication are from
the *Holy Bible, New International Version.*
Copyright © 1973, 1978, 1984 by the International Bible Society.
Published in North America by Zondervan Corporation.

Cover photo: Alan Bedding

Printed in Singapore

Contents

Preface

It would be impossible to stop Christians singing. One of the sure signs of the fullness of the Holy Spirit is to "sing and make music in your heart to the Lord" (Ephesians 5:18, 19). Especially when we come together to worship, our praises would be inconceivable without songs. So we say to one another, "Come, let us sing for joy to the Lord, let us shout aloud to the Rock of our Salvation" (Psalm 95:1).

In every generation new hymns have been written and published. Yet the oldest hymnbook of the church, the Psalter or Book of Psalms, has never lost its appeal.

Jesus himself loved the Psalms. He often quoted them. He also applied some of them to himself. He was David's son and lord (Psalm 110), he said, and the rejected stone which became the builder's capstone (Psalm 118). He also saw himself as experiencing the terrible sufferings of the innocent victim who is depicted, for example, in Psalms 22, 31, 41 and 59.

The reason why Christian people are drawn to the psalms is that they speak the universal language of the human soul. "The Book of Psalms," wrote Rowland E. Prothero in *The Psalms in Human Life* (1904) "contains the whole music of the heart of man." Whatever our spiritual mood may be, there is sure to be a psalm which reflects it—whether triumph or defeat, excitement or depression, joy or sorrow, praise or penitence, wonder or anger. Above all, the psalms declare the greatness of the living God as Creator, Sustainer, King, Lawgiver, Savior, Father, Shepherd, and Judge. As we come to know him better through the Psalter, we fall down and worship him.

A book called *The Canticles and Selected Psalms* was published in 1966 in Hodder and Stoughton's series of "Prayer Book Commentaries". It has long been out of print. I am therefore grateful to Tim Dowley for proposing the modernization and republication of some of the expositions in this edition.

John Stott
2003

5

Psalm 1

The Way of the Righteous and the Wicked

Jerome quoted the opinion of some that this first psalm is "the preface of the Holy Spirit" to the Psalter. It is certainly a very apt introduction. Two particular themes are found in it, which recur in many other psalms.

The first is the clear-cut distinction between *the righteous* and *the wicked*. The Bible as a whole, and specially the Wisdom Literature, divides humankind into these two absolute categories, and does not recognize a third. Psalms 32, 36, and 112 also compare and contrast the righteous and the wicked.

The second theme concerns the present fortunes and the ultimate destinies of human beings. The first and last words of Psalm 1 indicate the alternatives. *Blessed* is the righteous person who delights in God's law; the ungodly, on the other hand, will *perish*. This process of "blessing" and "cursing", as Jeremiah called it when he perhaps elaborated this psalm (see Jeremiah 17:5–8), is already discernible in this life.

In handling these two themes the author of Psalm 1 is only anticipating what Jesus Himself was to teach, that men and women are either on the broad road that leads to destruction or on the narrow way that leads to life (Matthew 7:13, 14).

---

¹Blessed is the man
  who who does not walk in
    the counsel of the wicked
or stand in the way of sinners
  or sit in the seat of mockers.
²But his delight is in the law of
    the LORD,
  and on his law he meditates
    day and night.
³He is like a tree planted by
    streams of water,
  which yield its fruit in season
and whose leaf does not wither.

Whatever he does prospers.
⁴Not so the wicked!
  They are like the chaff
  that the wind blows away.
⁵Therefore the wicked will not
    stand in the judgment,
  nor sinners in the assembly of
    the righteous.
⁶For the LORD watches over the
    way of the righteous,
but the way of the wicked will
    perish.

The righteous will prosper (vs 1–4)

The righteous person is described first negatively, then positively. He or she *does not walk in the counsel of the wicked or stand in the way of sinners or sit in the seat of mockers.* These expressions have been carefully composed in a triple set of parallels: "walk, stand, sit", "counsel, way, seat", and "wicked, sinners, mockers". Moreover, a downward progression is implied. The godly do not model their conduct on the advice of bad people. Further, the godly do not linger in the company of persistent evildoers; still less remain permanently among the cynical who openly scoff at God.

Instead of taking the lead from such people, the godly make *the law of the LORD* their rule (v 2). This *law (Torah)* refers not just to the Ten Commandments, or even all the rules and regulations of the law of Moses, but to all God's revelation as the guide of life, which, although given through Moses and the prophets, is yet *the law of the LORD,* a phrase virtually equivalent to "the word of God".

The law of the Lord is the righteous person's *delight.*This is an indication of new birth, for "...the sinful mind is hostile to God. It does not submit to God's law, nor can it do so" (Romans 8:7). As a result of the inward, regenerating work of the Holy Spirit, however, the godly find that they love the law of God simply because it conveys to them the will of their God. They do not rebel against its exacting demands; their whole being approves and endorses it (see Psalms 19; 40:8; 112:1; 119). Delighting in it, the godly will *meditate* in it, or pore over it, constantly, day and night.

It is believed that this was the favorite text of Jerome, the author of the old Latin version of the Bible. He certainly exemplified it in his life, relentlessly pursuing his study of the Scriptures first in the desert, and then for nearly 35 years in his grotto near the traditional scene of the Nativity in Bethlehem. Indeed, all Christians know something of the psalmist's experience. To them daily meditation in the Bible is an unending delight.

This, then, is the characteristic of the righteous. For guidance regarding daily conduct they look not to public opinion, the unreliable fashions of the godless world, but to the revealed Word of God, in which they delight and meditate. As a result they are *like a tree planted by streams of water* (v 3).

The metaphor is a common one in the Bible. Whatever kind of tree is in mind, it clearly enjoys the secret of perennial health and vigor, its fruit ripening in its season, and its leaf not withering even under the heat of the sun; for as the tree draws constant nourishment from the water through its roots, so through daily meditation in the law of the Lord the righteous refresh and replenish their soul in God. Such a tree is firmly *planted*; such people, like Joshua, prosper in whatever they do.

The ungodly will perish (vs 5, 6)

Not so the wicked! Their present condition and future destiny are entirely different. Instead of being like a fruitful tree, they are like dry and useless chaff. Instead of being planted by the waterside, they are driven by the wind.

Again, the metaphor was a familiar one in Bible days and Bible lands (compare Psalm 35:5; Isaiah 17:13; Matthew 3:12). The threshing floor was usually a hard, flat surface situated on a hill, well exposed to the wind. The wheat was lifted by large winnowing fans or shovels and thrown into the air, so that the precious grain would drop down and be garnered, while the light husks of the chaff would be scattered to the four winds.

The wicked *are like chaff* in two senses. They are desiccated and unprofitable in themselves; and they are easily blown away by the judgment of God. The basic idea behind the Hebrew word for *the wicked* appears to be one of "restlessness" (compare Isaiah 57:20, 21). The tree is planted firmly; but the chaff is unstable. When God begins to sift them in his present activity of judgment, and specially when the final day of judgment comes, they will not stand. Not even now can they stand *in the assembly of the righteous*, for they do not belong to the godly remnant of his people.

Verse 6 is a general conclusion to the whole psalm, distinguishing between *the way of the righteous* and *the way of the wicked*. We are told that the Lord *watches over the way of the righteous*; whereas *the way of the wicked will perish*.

Psalm 8

What is a Human Being?

"This short, exquisite lyric," as it was called by C. S. Lewis, begins and ends with the refrain: *O Lord, our Lord, how majestic is your name in all the earth.* Here is a recognition of the majesty of God's name, or nature, which his works reveal in both earth and heaven. The enemies of God, blinded by their proud rebellion, do not see his glory; but they are confounded by *children and infants.* Jesus quoted these words when the children acclaimed him in the Temple with their hosannas, while the chief priests and scribes indignantly objected (Matthew 21:15, 16). God is still glorified in the simple faith of children and in the childlike humility of Christian believers (see Matthew 11:25, 26; 1 Corinthians 1:26–29).

What particularly evokes the wondering worship of the psalmist is God's condescension toward human beings (vs 3, 4) and the position of dominion which he has granted to them on

---

¹O Lord, our Lord,
  how majestic is your name in
    all the earth!
You have set your glory
  above the heavens.
²From the lips of children and
    infants
  you have ordained praise
because of your enemies,
  to silence the foe and the
    avenger.
³When I consider your heavens,
  the work of your fingers,
the moon and the stars,
  which you have set in place,
⁴what is man that you are
    mindful of him,
  the son of man that you care
    for him?

⁵You made him a little lower
    than the heavenly beings
  and crowned him with glory
    and honor.
⁶You made him ruler over the
    works of your hands;
  you put everything under his
    feet:
⁷all flocks and herds,
  and beasts of the field,
⁸the birds of the air,
  and fish of the sea,
  all that swim the paths of the
    seas.
⁹O Lord, our Lord,
  how majestic is your name in
    all the earth!

---

earth (vs 5–8). Seen in relation to each other, these two truths enable us to have a balanced judgment of humankind and to give a proper answer to the psalmist's rhetorical question, *What is man?* (v 4), that is, What does it mean to be a human being?

The littleness of human beings (vs 3, 4)

The question was prompted by a consideration of the night sky. If David was the author of this psalm, there can be little doubt that he was referring to the experience of his youth. In his shepherd days, tending his father's flocks in the hills near Bethlehem, he often slept under the stars. Lying on his back, he would survey the fathomless immensity above him, seeking to penetrate the clear depths of the eastern sky. He recognized that the heavens, with the moon and the stars, were the work of God's fingers (v 3), and as he contemplated their greatness and mystery, he cried out: *What is man that you are mindful of him, and the son of man that you care for him?* (v 4).

If this was David's reaction, nearly 3,000 years ago, how much more should it be ours who live in days of astro-physics and the conquest of space? As we consider the orbiting planets of our solar system, so infinitesimally small in comparison with countless galaxies millions of light years distant, it may seem to us incredible that the great God of the universe should take any note of us at all, let alone *care for us.* Yet he does; and Jesus assured us that even the hairs of our head are all numbered.

The greatness of human beings (vs 5–8)

The psalmist moves from the littleness of a human being, in comparison with the vastness of the universe, to the greatness which God has given him on earth: *You made him a little lower than the heavenly beings and crowned him with glory and honor. You made him ruler over the works of your hands* (vs 5, 6).

Our position of only slight inferiority to the heavenly beings, or even to God himself, is supremely seen in our *rule.* God has invested human beings with royal sovereignty, crowning us with glory and honor (v 5) and delegating to us the control of his works. It is even stated that God has put *everything...under his* (man's) *feet.*

The psalmist is referring primarily to the animal creation—beasts both domesticated and wild, *the birds of the air, and the fish of the sea*, and all other creatures inhabiting the depths of the ocean (vs 7, 8). This is not poetic fiction. As the universe yields more and more of its secrets to scientific research, so our dominion increases. Yet even now humankind is not, in fact, lord of creation, with *everything* under our feet, as is recognized in the three New Testament quotations of these verses.

According to Hebrews 2:5 and the following verses: "...at present we do not see everything subject to him." It is immediately added, however: "But we see Jesus, who was made a little lower than the angels, now crowned with glory and honor." Humankind has sinned and fallen, and consequently has lost some of the dominion which God had given us; but in Jesus, the second Adam, this dominion has been restored. It is in him rather than in us that humankind's dominion is exhibited. By his death he even destroyed the devil and delivered his slaves (vs 14, 15). He has now been "crowned", and exalted to God's right hand.

Although the Psalm's description of humankind's dominion is true rather of the man Christ Jesus than of us, it applies to us also if we have come by faith to share in his exaltation. The apostle Paul wrote that the exceeding greatness of God's power, which exalted Jesus and "put everything under his feet", is available to us who believe (Ephesians 1:19–22). Indeed, we have experienced it, for it has raised us from the death of sin, exalted us with Christ and made us sit with him in the heavenly places, where we are partakers of his victory and dominion (Ephesians 2:5, 6).

Even this is not the end. Although Christ is exalted far above all rule and authority, and all things are potentially under his feet, not all his enemies have yet conceded their defeat or surrendered to him. Only when he appears in glory and the dead rise, will he destroy "all dominion, authority and power. For he must reign until he has put all his enemies under his feet. The last enemy to be destroyed is death. For he 'has put everything under his feet'" (1 Corinthians 15:24–26).

Psalm 15

An Uncorrupt Life

Psalm 15 is concerned with the conditions on which a man or woman may dwell with God. It is especially noteworthy because it units religion and morality in an undissoluble partnership. It opens with a question, continues with an answer to the question posed, and concludes with a grand assertion which goes beyond the terms of the original question.

The question (v 1)

Lord, who may dwell in your sanctuary? Who may live on your holy hill? God's *holy hill* was of course Jerusalem and his *sanctuary* probably the tent which housed the ark before Solomon built the Temple. Indeed, it has generally been thought that this psalm, like Psalm 24, refers to the occasion, described in 2 Samuel 6:12–19 and 1 Chronicles 15 and 16, when David brought the ark from the house of Obed-edom on to Mount Zion, "the city of David", and placed it in the tent which he had pitched for it. In this case, the psalm outlines the moral challenge which God's presence in their midst brought to the inhabitants of Jerusalem.

---

¹LORD, who may dwell in your sanctuary?
Who may live on your holy hill?
²He whose walk is blameless
and who does what is righteous,
who speaks the truth from his heart
³ and has no slander on his tongue,
who does his neighbor no wrong
and casts no slur on his fellow man,
⁴who despises a vile man
but honors those who fear the LORD,
who keeps his oath
even when it hurts,
⁵who lends his money without usury
and does not accept a bribe against the innocent.
He who does these things
will never be shaken.

But the psalm has a wider application than this. It inquires into the terms on which any human being may dwell in God's presence, either in this life or in the life to come. The psalmist is clear that Jehovah is a holy God and that sinners separate themselves from God by their sin. "You are not a God who takes pleasure in evil; with you the wicked cannot dwell" (Psalm 5:4). Who, then, may dwell with God?

The answer (vs 2–6)

The psalmist now answers his own question and describes the kind of person who may draw near to God. He paints an attractive picture. Indeed, no one has perfectly fulfilled this ideal except the man Christ Jesus. Jesus Christ alone has entered the presence of God in heaven in virtue of his own merit; for us access to God is possible only through Christ.

But, having been brought near to God by Christ, we can enjoy continuing fellowship with him only if by his grace we lead the kind of holy life which this psalm depicts. It is a social holiness. That is, it concerns entirely our duty to our neighbor, since we cannot have a right relationship with God without a right relationship with human beings. We cannot expect to dwell in God's presence if we are not seeking our neighbor's good.

So the people who may enjoy God's company are described as *blameless* (v 2). They are people of such complete integrity of character that they both do what is right and speak what is true. Further, the truth they speak is from their *heart*, for they always mean what they say. They are thus consistent in thought, word, and deed.

This general and positive statement is now illustrated by particular and largely negative examples. Indeed, it is against the background of these negatives that the positive excellence of good people stands out in shining relief.

First, they do not harm their neighbors by anything they say or do (v 3). They neither slander them, nor wrong them, nor cast slurs against them. This last expression probably means either that they do not repeat gossip about their neighbors, or that they do not take unfair advantage of them when they are overtaken by adversity. Secondly, they are discerning in their assessment of others (v 4). They are not afraid to express disapproval of worthless people. Thirdly, they are faithful to their promises, even when it is to their own inconvenience or disadvantage. They are people of their word (v 5). Fourthly, they never exploit the poor or oppress the innocent (v 6).

More precisely, they do not lend money on usury or accept bribes. We are introduced here to familiar figures in the Old Testament—the extortionate moneylender and the unjust magistrate who perverts justice for a bribe. Both practices were forbidden by the law (Exodus 22:25; Leviticus 25:35–38 and Exodus 23:6–8; Deuteronomy 16:19; 27:25) and denounced by the prophets (see, for example, Ezekiel 22:12).

The assertion (v 7)

The psalmist has asked who shall dwell in God's presence, and has answered his own question by portraying a person who loves his or her neighbor. But he does not stop there. Such people, he concludes, will not only abide in God's sanctuary; they *will never be shaken*. On the contrary, they will remain firm and secure throughout all the vicissitudes of this life, and on the day of judgment.

Psalm 16

Present Faith and Future Hope

Although this psalm opens with a prayer (*Keep me safe, O God*), it is in reality a believer's testimony regarding both his present faith and his future hope. Having taken refuge in God (v 1), he has found in Him his greatest good (vs 2, 6, 7) and is convinced that even death cannot rob him of that true life which consists of fellowship with God (vs 11, 12). These final verses were applied to the resurrection of Jesus Christ by Peter on the day of Pentecost and by Paul in the synagogue of Antioch in Pisidia (Acts 2:24–31; 13: 34–37).

---

¹Keep me safe, O God,
   for in you I take refuge.
²I said to the LORD, "You are my Lord;
   apart from you I have no good thing."
³As for the saints who are in the land,
   they are the glorious ones in whom is all my delight.
⁴The sorrows of those will increase
   who run after other gods.
I will not pour out their libations of blood
   or take up their names on my lips.
⁵LORD, you have assigned me my portion and my cup;
   you have made my lot secure.
⁶The boundary lines have fallen for me in pleasant places;
   surely I have a delightful inheritance.

⁷I praise the LORD, who counsels me;
   even at night my heart instructs me.
⁸I have set the LORD always before me.
   Because he is at my right hand, I shall not be shaken.
⁹Therefore my heart is glad and my tongue rejoices;
   my body also will rest secure,
¹⁰because you will not abandon me to the grave,
   nor will you let your Holy One see decay.
¹¹You have made known to me the path of life;
   you will fill me with joy in your presence,
   with eternal pleasures at your right hand.

Present faith (vs 1–6)

What it means to put one's trust in God, or to *take refuge* (v 1) in him, is explained in verse 2 (compare Psalm 73:24). The believer has turned from the pleasures of sin and the vanities of the world to seek and find his good in God. Delighting in God, he delights also in the godly, the *saints* (v 3).

In the ungodly, however, who have exchanged the true and living God for *other gods* (v 4), the believer takes no delight. He knows that they will have great trouble—their *sorrows…will increase*. He affirms with resolve that he will neither offer their idolatrous libations of blood nor even mention the names of their false deities (v 5). To do so would be incompatible with his wholehearted devotion to the Lord, of whom he now writes in the most exalted terms (vs 5, 6). The Lord has assigned him his *portion* (alluding probably to a portion of food rather than of land) and his *cup*, thus both satisfying his hunger and quenching his thirst. Further, he has found God to be a *delightful inheritance*, just like the Levitical priests, who were given no inheritance in Canaan because their inheritance was the Lord (see, for example, Numbers 18:20).

Future hope (vs 7–11)

David, who according to the apostles Peter and Paul was the author of this psalm, now breaks out into thanksgiving (v 7) that the Lord has given him *counsel* and that at *night* his *heart instructs* him. What this divine instruction is which he has received he does not make clear. It seems best to refer it to the remaining verses of the psalm.

God draws near to David and speaks to him; his own heart teaches him while in the stillness of the night he meditates on his intimate fellowship with God. He learns to draw from his experience this mighty deduction: that because God is ever before him and beside him (v 8), *I shall not be shaken*. In other words, the blessings of his communion with God cannot be limited to his satisfaction only; they include his security also. His present faith brings a future hope.

David now rejoices in heart and soul because he is convinced that his body also may *rest secure* (v 9). He goes on to elaborate his new assurance in direct speech to God (vs 11, 12).

Three levels of interpretation are possible in these verses, all of which are true. Literally they express the writer's confidence that he will not die, that his soul will not be delivered *to the grave*—the translation of the Hebrew *sheol*, the abode of the dead. Nor will his body *see decay*. We do not know the historical circumstances in which the psalm was written, but it may possibly express the confidence which sustained David during his months as an outlaw, that he would not be delivered into the hand of Saul.

The implication of these verses goes further than this, however. The corollary to deliverance from death is treading *the path of life*; and this life is seen to be no mere physical survival, but the enjoyment of God's presence bringing *joy* and *eternal pleasures*. It is in fact what the New Testament calls "eternal life", communion with God, which physical death cannot interrupt. It is unlikely that David understood fully what he was writing, since life and immortality were only clearly revealed by Jesus Christ (2 Timothy 1:10); yet his words find their true fulfillment only in the consummation of eternal life beyond the grave.

When Peter applied these verses to the resurrection of Jesus, he went so far as to say that David cannot have been referring primarily to himself, since he died and was buried. He went on: "But he was a prophet and knew that God had promised him on oath that he would place one of his descendants on his throne. Seeing what was ahead, he spoke of the resurrection of the Christ, that he was not abandoned to the grave, nor did his body see decay" (Acts 2:30, 31).

We must be careful not to make Peter say more than he actually did say. He himself in his first letter (1 Peter 1:10–12) explained that the prophets did not fully understand to what the Spirit of Christ within them was referring when predicting Christ's sufferings and subsequent glory. We need not therefore assert that David was making a deliberate and conscious prophecy of the resurrection of Jesus which was fully intelligible to himself. It is enough to say that, caught up by the Spirit of prophecy, he was led to write words about the conquest of death and the fulness of life and joy in the presence of God, which would be finally fulfilled not in his own experience but in that of his illustrious descendant.

Psalm 19

The Self-Revelation of God

According to C. S. Lewis, this is "the greatest poem in the Psalter and one of the greatest lyrics in the world." From the Christian point of view it contains the clearest summary of the doctrine of revelation to be found in the Old Testament, namely that God

¹The heavens declare the glory
  of God;
  the skies proclaim the work of
  his hands.
²Day after day they pour forth
  speech;
  night after night they display
  knowledge.
³There is no speech or language
  where their voice is not heard.
⁴Their voice goes out into all the
  earth,
  their words to the ends of the
  world.
In the heavens he has pitched a
  tent for the sun,
⁵which is like a bridegroom
  coming forth from his
  pavilion,
  like a champion rejoicing to
  run his course.
⁶It rises at one end of the heavens
  and makes its circuit to the
  other;
  nothing is hidden from its heat.
⁷The Law of the LORD is perfect,
  reviving the soul.
The statutes of the LORD are
  trustworthy,
  making wise the simple.
⁸The precepts of the LORD are
  right,

giving joy to the heart.
The commands of the LORD are
  radiant,
  giving light to the eyes.
⁹The fear of the LORD is pure;
  enduring for ever.
The ordinances of the LORD are
  sure
  and altogether righteous.
¹⁰They are more precious than
  gold,
  than much pure gold;
they are sweeter than honey,
  than honey from the comb.
¹¹By them is your servant warned;
  in keeping them there is great
  reward.
¹²Who can discern his errors?
  Forgive my hidden faults.
¹³Keep your servant also from
  wilful sins;
  may they not rule over me.
Then will I be blameless,
  innocent of the great
  transgression.
¹⁴May the words of my mouth and
  the meditation of my heart
  be pleasing in your sight,
  O LORD, my Rock and my
  Redeemer.

has made himself known to all humankind as Creator (vs 1–6), to Israel as Lawgiver (vs 7–10), and to the individual as Redeemer (vs 11–14).

General revelation (vs 1–6)

Human beings cannot plead ignorance of God, since he never ceases to give a revelation of himself, which is called "general" because it is made to all people everywhere. As the apostle Paul put it, he has not "left himself without testimony" (Acts 14:17; compare Acts 17:22–28 and Romans 1:20).

This witness is in nature, especially here the *heavens*, which *declare the glory of God* because they are *the work of his hands* (v 1). Even more today, through the cosmology of modern astrophysics, the heavens, "their vastness, splendor, order and mystery" as one commentator puts it, reveal God's glory and greatness.

God's witness to himself through the heavens has three characteristics. First, it is continuous. *Day after day...night after night* (v 2) the testimony is given without intermission. Secondly, it is abundant. The verb in verse 2 is expressive: *they* (the heavens) *pour forth speech*. Thirdly it is universal. Although *there is no speech or language* (v 3), yet by sight rather than sound their message penetrates to the end of the world (v 4). Paul even applies this last verse to the worldwide spread of the gospel (Romans 10:18).

Of this universal witness to God by the heavens, the sun is a particular example. In dramatic imagery, which is not of course intended to be taken literally, the psalmist likens the sunrise to the emergence of a bridegroom from his chamber, and its daily course across the sky to the running of an athlete, so that *nothing is hidden from its heat* (v 6).

Special revelation (vs 7–10)

Abruptly and without warning the subject changes from God's general and natural revelation through creation to his special and supernatural revelation through *torah*, "the law", which refers not merely to the law of Moses but to all Old Testament Scripture. The transition, though abrupt, is not arbitrary. The heavens and the law both make God known. Further, C. S. Lewis may be right to detect a link in the reference to the all-pervasive heat of the sun, so that "the searching and cleansing sun becomes an image of the searching and cleansing law."

With the change of subject comes a significant change in the divine name. The One who reveals himself in nature to all people is *God*, Hebrew *El* (v 1), the God of creation; but it is the LORD Yahweh (seven times in the second half of the psalm), the God of the covenant, who has revealed himself through his law to his covenant people Israel. It is a revelation not now of his glory but of his will, and its excellencies are set forth in perfect Hebrew parallelism (vs 7–9).

The symmetry of these verses is so precise that each begins with a different aspect of God's will, and goes on to describe both what it is and what it does. Thus, *the law*, or divine instruction, is *perfect*, bearing witness to God's nature expressed in his will, and consists of particular *statutes*, *precepts*, and *commands*. Its perfection is seen in the fact that its injunctions are *trustworthy, right, radiant, pure, sure and altogether righteous*. It is also called *the fear of the LORD* (v 9) because the great end of all revelation is to inspire a humble and reverent worship of God. This disclosure of God's will is said to be *pure*.

But the psalmist does not merely contemplate the law of the Lord as it is in itself; he also unfolds its beneficial effects, *reviving the soul*, rejoicing the heart and, above all, *making wise* (v 7) and *giving light* (v 8) to those who are humble enough, or (as our Lord was later to teach) childlike enough, to receive it. The inherent qualities and health-giving results of God's law make it *more precious than gold. . . sweeter. . . than honey from the comb* (v 10).

It may be surprising to us that the writer did not find God's law a burden to him; we may feel with C. S. Lewis that his reference to its sweetness is at first sight "very mysterious", even "utterly bewildering". The explanation is not just that its commandments were right, nor that its promises were sure, but that it was the revelation of God, the special means which he had chosen to make himself known to his people Israel.

Personal revelation (vs 11–14)

With verse 11 the psalmist for the first time mentions himself. He has been describing how *all the earth* (v 4) may apprehend God's glory from nature, and how *the simple* (v 7) may derive wisdom from God's law. But he concludes his psalm by disclosing his personal spiritual aspirations as God's *servant* (vs 11, 13).

He has himself found wholesome warning in God's law and knows that conformity to it brings great reward (v 11). He seems to have discovered in his own experience the dual purpose of the divine law, namely to reveal sin (Romans 3:20) and to promote holiness. This leads him both to pray for cleansing from the *hidden faults* (v 12) which he has committed, and for deliverance from *wilful sins* (v 13) which he longs to avoid, so that he is not mastered by them but is kept *innocent of great transgression*. The psalmist is not referring here to any one particularly grievous sin, or even the blasphemy against the Holy Spirit (as poor John Bunyan thought), but to all deliberate wrongdoing, sins committed "defiantly" (Numbers 15:30, 31).

The psalm ends with a prayer which is frequently echoed by Christian ministers before they preach. In it the writer goes beyond his plea for deliverance, to a positive and very personal desire that all his words, and even his thoughts, shall be *pleasing* in the sight of God, whom he now declares to be both his *Rock* ("strength") and his *Redeemer*. Redemption is in itself negative deliverance from sin; it needs to be completed by a life that is pleasing to God (see Titus 2:14).

Psalm 22

The Sufferings and Glory of Christ

¹My God, my God, why have you
forsaken me?
Why are you so far from saving
me,
so far from the words of my
groaning?
²O my God, I cry out by day, but
you do not answer,
by night, and am not silent.
³Yet you are enthroned as the
Holy One;
you are the praise of Israel.
⁴In you our fathers put their trust;
they trusted you and you
delivered them.
⁵They cried to you and were saved;
in you they trusted and were
not disappointed.
⁶But I am a worm and not a man,
scorned by men and despised
by people.
⁷All who see me mock me;
they hurl insults, shaking their
heads:
⁸"He trusts in the LORD;
let the LORD rescue him.
Let him deliver him,
since he delights in him."
⁹Yet you brought me out of the
womb;
you made me trust in you
even at my mother's breast.
¹⁰From my birth I was cast upon
you;
from my mother's womb you
have been my God.
¹¹Do not be far from me,
for trouble is near

and there is no-one to help.
¹²Many bulls surround me;
strong bulls of Bashan encircle
me.
¹³Roaring lions tearing their prey
open their mouths wide against
me.
¹⁴I am poured out like water,
and all my bones are out of
joint.
My heart has turned to wax;
it has melted away within me.
¹⁵My strength is dried up like a
potsherd,
and my tongue sticks to the
root of my mouth;
you lay me in the dust of death.
¹⁶Dogs have surrounded me;
a band of evil men has encircled
me,
they have pierced my hands
and feet.
¹⁷I can count all my bones;
people stare and gloat over me.
¹⁸They divide my garments among
them
and cast lots for my clothing.
¹⁹But you, O LORD, be not far off;
O my Strength, come quickly
to help me.
²⁰Deliver my life from the sword,
my precious life from the
power of the dogs.
²¹Rescue me from the mouth of
the lions;
save me from the horns of wild
oxen.
²²I will declare your name to my

brothers;
in the congregation I will praise you.
²³You who fear the LORD, praise him!
All you descendants of Jacob, honor him!
Revere him, all you descendants of Israel!
²⁴For he has not despised or disdained
the suffering of the afflicted one;
he has not hidden his face from him
but has listened to his cry for help.
²⁵From you comes my praise in the great assembly;
before those who fear you, will I fulfil my vows.
²⁶The poor will eat and be satisfied;
they who seek the LORD will

praise him—
may your hearts live for ever!
²⁷All the ends of the earth
will remember and turn to the LORD,
and all the families of the nations will bow down before him,
²⁸for dominion belongs to the LORD,
and he rules over nations.
²⁹All the rich of the earth will feast and worship;
all who go down to the dust will kneel before him—
those who cannot keep themselves alive.
³⁰Posterity will serve him;
future generations will be told about the LORD.
³¹They will proclaim his righteousness
to a people yet unborn—
for he has done it.

This is the first of a number of so-called "passion psalms" in the Psalter, which describe the suffering and persecution of an innocent victim in terms reminiscent of the Suffering Servant of the Lord in the second part of Isaiah. Although some commentators have suggested that the godly sufferer is more ideal than real, representing perhaps the Israelite nation when exiled among the heathen, the narrative of his afflictions is so vivid in its details that it undoubtedly depicts a true and literal experience.

Yet Christian eyes cannot read this psalm, nor Christian lips sing it, without applying it to the sufferings of Christ and his subsequent glory. Not only did Jesus quote its opening words as one of his seven sayings from the cross (Matthew 27:46; Mark 15:34), but the mockery of verses 7 and 8 was echoed by the priests (Matthew 27:39–44; Mark 15:31–32; Luke 23:35), the division of clothing in verse 18 was said to be fulfilled by the soldiers (John 19:23, 24), and verse 22 is applied to Christ in Hebrews 2:11, 12. Further, the sufferer's agony in verses 14 to 17 —his disjointed bones, his thirst and his pierced hands and feet —is a remarkable description of the horrors of crucifixion, although it is not quoted of Christ in the New Testament.

The psalm is in two contrasting parts.

The cry of anguish (vs 1–21)

The sufferer cries out to God in an agonized question: *Why have you forsaken me?* His greatest suffering is neither the physical pain, nor the mockery of his persecutors, which he will later describe, but his sense of God-forsakenness. His question is asked in perplexity, not in despair or bitterness. Indeed, the poignancy of his condition is that he continues in faith to appeal to God three times as *my God* even while he is forsaken and receives no reply.

Three thoughts seem to aggravate his condition and at the same time buttress his faith. He expresses them in the next paragraphs. First, there was the experience of the ancients (vs 3–5). He knows that God is *holy*, separate from and exalted above all other beings, because the fathers trusted in him and cried to him, and they were delivered, *not disappointed*. Secondly, there are the taunts of his enemies, (vs 6–8), who mock him because his experience is not like that of the fathers: *He trusts in the LORD; let the LORD rescue him.* Will God allow them thus to blaspheme him? Thirdly, the psalmist looks back to his own past experience of God (vs 9–11). Jehovah has been his God from his birth; he will surely not abandon him now. These thoughts lead him to a piteous appeal to God (v 11) that he will not be far away, since trouble is close at hand.

What precisely is his *trouble*? He is evidently very sick, indeed dying, fast approaching *the dust of death* (v 15). He portrays the physical symptoms he both sees and feels (vs 14, 15).

But his bodily pains are made worse by the *band of evil men* (v 16) who surround him. He has already likened them to *strong bulls* from the rich pasture-land of Bashan and to lions ready to devour him (vs 12, 13). Now he pictures them as savage pariah *dogs* (v 16), and later as *wild oxen* (v 21) waiting to tear him limb from limb. In some brutal way they pierce his hands and feet; they *stare and gloat* over him (v 17); they even strip him of his clothes and share them out (v 18), or have done so mentally in anticipation of his death. For the third time (see verses 1, 2, and 11) he appeals to God to draw near to him in his need and to deliver him (vs 19–21).

The song of praise (vs 22–31)

Suddenly and dramatically the tone of the psalm changes from prayer to praise, from suffering to triumph. God's deliverance of the sufferer is not described. We are simply told (v 24) that in the end God has *not despised* his afflicted servant, as men had despised him (v 6), but has heard his cry when he called to him. The psalmist's soul is so transported with adoration that he wants everybody to praise God with him. The true worshiper is always thus missionary-minded; he cannot conceive of praising God alone. In the remaining verses of the psalm the circle of those who are summoned to the worship of God grows ever wider until finally it embraces all nations and all ages.

First, he will declare and praise God's name in the great assembly (vs 22–25). He means to bear public witness to God's deliverance among his fellow Israelites, the *descendants of Jacob*, and offer him public praise. Next, he seems to think of his fellow-sufferers, others who are still *poor* (v 26) or "afflicted" (Revised Standard Version) as he has been (v 24). He wants them to share his joy and with him *eat and be satisfied*, probably in the sacrificial meal which followed a thank-offering. Next (vs 27, 28) his prophetic eyes look on to the conversion of the nations, and he asserts that *All the ends of the earth will…turn to the Lord*, recognizing that universal *dominion belongs* to him.

Even this glorious prospect does not exhaust his vision. Although verse 29 is acknowledged as obscure and may bring together either the proud and the humble who realize their mortality, or the living and the dead, yet verses 30 and 31 contain a clear reference to the psalmist's *posterity*. They too, *a people yet unborn*, shall hear of the Lord and of his salvation. Thus, the publishing of the gospel of salvation is to be both universal and everlasting, and we see dimly foreshadowed in the results of this godly man's sufferings the final triumph of the Crucified.

Psalm 23

The Lord is My Shepherd

There are, in this best known and best loved of all psalms, two graphic pictures of God's intimate relationship with one of his people. The first is the shepherd and his sheep, the second the host and his guest.

The Lord my shepherd (vs 1–4)

It was natural for a pastoral community to think of the Lord as their shepherd, who *brought his people out like a flock; he led them like sheep through the desert* (Psalm 78:52; see also Psalm 80:1; Isaiah 40:11). But here the metaphor is made unmistakably personal. *The Lord is my shepherd*, the writer boldly claims, and does not even mention the other sheep of the flock.

The Christian cannot read or sing this psalm without thinking of Jesus Christ, who dared to reapply the metaphor from Jehovah to himself. It is he who is to us "the good shepherd", "the Chief Shepherd", and "that great Shepherd of the sheep" (John 10:11, 14; 1 Peter 5:4; Hebrews 13:20).

Once I can say from personal experience *the Lord is my shepherd*, I can add with assurance the consequence: *I shall lack*

---

¹The Lord is my shepherd, I shall lack nothing.
²He makes me lie down in green pastures,
he leads me beside quiet waters,
³ he restores my soul.
He guides me in paths of righteousness
for his name's sake.
⁴Even though I walk through the valley of the shadow of death,
I will fear no evil,

for you are with me;
your rod and staff,
they comfort me.
⁵You prepare a table before me
in the presence of my enemies.
You anoint my head with oil;
my cup overflows.
⁶Surely goodness and love will follow me
all the days of my life,
and I will dwell in the house of the Lord for ever.

---

nothing. The Good Shepherd cares for his sheep and so provides for all my needs. He makes me lie down in green pastures to satisfy my hunger, and leads me beside refreshing waters to quench my thirst (v 2). *For his name's sake,* that is, out of loyalty to his character and promises, he will guide me *in the paths of righteousness;* that is, he will not allow me to go astray (v 3).

Indeed, even when I walk *through the darkest valley* (alternative translation, verse 4), whether that be death or some other somber place, I have nothing to fear and I will not fear, because my Shepherd is *with me,* protecting me with his club and guiding me with his staff (v 4). My security lies not, then, in my environment—whether green pastures and still waters or the darkest valley—but in my Shepherd. In his presence there is neither want (v 1) nor fear (v 4).

The Lord my host (vs 5, 6)

The scene changes. I am no longer out of doors, but indoors; no longer a sheep in a flock, but a guest at a banquet. My divine host has prepared *a table before me.* It is not a secret feast, but enjoyed in the presence of my enemies, because when he satisfies the soul, it cannot be hidden from the world.

His provision is wonderfully lavish—a table laden with food, perfumed oils to anoint my head, and an overflowing cup (v 5). Moreover, what God has begun he will surely continue. As he himself will *lead me* (vs 2, 3), so his *goodness and love will follow me.* Thus he will guard me behind and before, throughout *all the days of my life.* Finally, *I will dwell in the house of the Lord for ever*—not indeed in the Tabernacle or the Temple, nor even just in his presence in this life, but in that Father's house with its many mansions, of which Jesus spoke, where he said he was going to prepare a place for his own (John 14:1–4).

Psalm 24

Ascending the Hill of the Lord

The most probable historical setting for this psalm is the triumphant occasion described in 2 Samuel 6 when King David brought the ark from the house of Obed-edom into the tent which he had pitched for it in Jerusalem. It is probable that an annual Jewish festival commemorated either this event or God's choice of David and of Jerusalem, and that during it the ark was carried into the city and this psalm was sung.

Whatever the occasion, it is not difficult to imagine a processional choir singing it as they approached the Temple on Mount Zion, with the questions and answers of verses 3 and 4, and 7 to 10, chanted antiphonally as is sometimes done with effect by choirs today.

The whole earth (vs 1, 2)

The psalm opens with a grand statement that the whole earth, with all its inhabitants, belongs to the Lord (v 1) because he is its creator (v 2): he has *founded it upon the seas* and *established it upon the waters*. This description of the land floating on the sea is of course poetic and is perhaps based on the account in Genesis 1 of the appearance of the dry land out of the sea. It is not misleading even today (figuratively speaking) when we consider that about 70 percent of the earth's surface consists of water. The statement in verse 1 that the earth and its contents belong to God is quoted by Paul in 1 Corinthians 10:26 to support his argument that Christians may eat any food, even idol meats.

The Lord's hill (vs 3–6)

Although the whole earth is the Lord's, there is a certain hill which is his in a special sense. Called *the hill of the LORD* (v 3) and *his holy place*, it is Mount Zion where the ark, the symbol of his presence, was housed. But *who may ascend* there into his holy presence (v 3)? The answer, which is reminiscent of Psalm 15,

---

¹The earth is the LORD's, and
      everything in it,
   the world, and all who live in it;
²for he founded it upon the seas
   and established it upon the
      waters.
³Who may ascend the hill of the
      LORD?
   Who may stand in his holy
      place?
⁴He who has clean hands and a
      pure heart,
   who does not lift up his soul
      to an idol
   or swear by what is false.
⁵He will receive blessing from the
      LORD
   and vindication from God our
      Savior.

⁶Such is the generation of those
      who seek him,
   who seek your face, O God of
      Jacob.
                              Selah
⁷Lift up your heads, O you gates;
   be lifted up, you ancient doors,
   that the King of glory may
      come in.
⁸Who is the King of glory?
   the LORD strong and mighty,
   the LORD mighty in battle.
⁹Lift up your heads, O you gates;
   lift them up, you ancient doors,
   that the King of glory may
      come in.
¹⁰Who is he, this King of glory?
   The LORD Almighty—
   he is the King of glory.
                              Selah

---

expresses that union of worship and morality which is constantly insisted on in the Bible.

The only worship which is acceptable to God is that offered by people who have *clean hands and a pure heart* (v 4), that is, who are holy in thought and motive as well as in deed. Moreover, their holiness characterizes their relationship with both God and others, for they do not *lift up (their) soul to an idol*, nor have they sworn *by what is false*, deceiving their neighbor. It is such people, godly and just, who will receive God's blessing and acceptance (v 5); indeed, such blessing is the portion of all those *who seek your face, O God of Jacob* (v 6).

The city gates (vs 7–10)

The procession bearing the ark has now reached the gates of the city of David, and the voices of the choir ring out: *Lift up your heads, O you gates…that the King of glory may come in* (v 7). Back comes the challenge from inside the city: *Who is this King of glory?* to which the choir responds: *The LORD strong and mighty, the LORD mighty in battle* (v 8). The whole dialogue is then repeated word for word (vs 9, 10), except that in the final response *the King of glory* is now further described as *the LORD Almighty*. It is the first time that this title occurs in the Psalter, and it forms a splendid climax to this psalm.

Psalm 27

The Soul's Changing Moods

The assertions and petitions of this psalm are made against the background of many enemies. If David was its author (which there seems no adequate reason to question), the situation

¹The Lord is my light and my
  salvation—
  whom shall I fear?
The Lord is the stronghold of my
  life—
  of whom shall I be afraid?
²When evil men advance against
  me
  to devout my flesh,
when my enemies and my foes
  attack me,
  they will stumble and fall.
³Though an army besiege me,
  my heart will not fear;
though war break out against me,
  even then will I be confident.
⁴One thing I ask of the Lord,
  this is what I seek:
that I may dwell in the house of
  the Lord
all the days of my life,
to gaze upon the beauty of the
  Lord
  and to seek him in his temple.
⁵For in the day of trouble
  he will keep me safe in his
  dwelling;
he will hide me in the shelter of
  his tabernacle
  and set me high upon a rock.
⁶Then my head will be exalted
  above the enemies who
  surround me;
at his tabernacle will I sacrifice
  with shouts of joy;
  I will sing and make music to
  the Lord.
⁷Hear my voice when I call, O Lord;
  be merciful to me and answer
  me.
⁸My heart says of you, "Seek his
  face!"
  Your face, Lord, I will seek.
⁹Do not hide your face from me,
  do not turn your servant away
  in anger;
  you have been my helper.
Do not reject me or forsake me,
  O God my Savior.
¹⁰Thou my father and mother
  forsake me,
  the Lord will receive me.
¹¹Teach me your way, O Lord;
  lead me in a straight path
  because of my oppressors.
¹²Do not hand me over to the
  desire of my foes,
  for false witnesses rise up
  against me,
  breathing out violence.
¹³I am still confident of this:
  I will see the goodness of the
  Lord
  in the land of the living.
¹⁴Wait for the Lord;
  be strong and take heart
  and wait for the Lord.

described is likely to be either his pursuit by Saul or his flight from Absalom. In any case, the enemies are *evil men* (v 2), persecuting him for righteousness' sake, and seeking to harm him by physical violence and by slander (v 14). He likens them to wild beasts eager to tear him limb from limb (v 2).

Confidence in God (vs 1–7)

The psalm opens with one of the most sublime Old Testament affirmations of the security of God's people. *The LORD is my light*, to guide me, *my salvation*, to deliver me, and *the stronghold of my life*, in whom I take refuge. *Of whom*, then, *shall I be afraid?* It is a defiant, unanswerable question reminiscent of those at the end of Romans 8. Let David's enemies attack him, yet *they will stumble and fall* (v 2). Indeed (v 3), if a whole army should make war against him, *even then* he will be *confident*.

Many Christians, surrounded by foes, have drawn strength from these words. One such was James Hannington, first Bishop of Equatorial Africa. In October 1885, on reaching Lake Victoria Nyanza, he was seized and imprisoned. "Consumed with fever, and at times delirious with pain, devoured by vermin, menaced every moment by the prospect of death, he found strength in the Psalms." On October 28, the day before he died a martyr's death, he wrote in his journal: "I am quite broken down and brought low. Comforted by Psalm 27."

This steadfast assurance of one man against many foes is now further explained. It lies in the presence and the protection of God. David cherishes one desire above all others (v 4), namely to *dwell in the house of the LORD* all his life, so that he may both *gaze upon the beauty of the LORD* or "savor the sweetness of the Lord" and *seek him in his temple*.

It is most unlikely that we are intended to interpret this ambition literally. Only the priests lived in the precincts of God's house, whether what is here meant is the tabernacle at Shiloh or on Mount Zion, and David could not have aspired to the priesthood since he belonged to the tribe of Judah, not the tribe of Levi. So we must interpret the language figuratively as a noble longing to enjoy unbroken communion with God, in order to worship his glory and discern his will. Compare Psalm 23:5, 6 for a similar reference to the house of God.

It was through such a life of abiding in God that David knew he would be delivered. *In the day of trouble* God would protect him, as a tent gives the traveler shelter from the sun or a high rock safety from the floods (vs 5, 6). For such deliverance he will praise God in his Tabernacle (literally this time) with sacrifices and *shouts of joy* (v 6).

Crying to God (vs 8–16)

Suddenly everything is different. The main verbs change from the third person to the second and from a statement to a prayer. The mood alters too, as confident affirmation gives place to an anxious supplication to God. So abrupt and complete is the change that some commentators have ascribed the two halves of the Psalm to different authors, or, if to the same author, at least to different occasions and circumstances. Yet those who know something of the soul's moods, of the ebb and flow of faith, and of the alternating rhythm of praise and prayer, will see no necessity for this double ascription.

David prays, seeking not only God's ear, but his face (vs 7, 8). He is encouraged to do so because of God's own invitation. When God says: *Seek my face* (see margin), his heart responds: *Your face, LORD, I will seek.* True prayer is never a presumptuous approach to God, but rather a response to his gracious initiative. It is this assurance which prompts David to add: *Do not hide your face from me* (v 9). Although he seems to recognize that his sins deserve only God's displeasure, he is sure that God, who has been his help in the past, will not now cast him off (v 10). Even were his own parents to forsake him, he says, *the LORD will receive me* (v 10), or "adopt me as his child," as one commentator puts it. For the likeness of God's love in the Old Testament to the tender care of a father or mother see Psalm 103:13; Isaiah 49:15; 63:16.

The negative prayer not to be forsaken is now followed by a positive petition for guidance, that his steps may be directed on to a level path. He desires to be taught God's way (v 13), lest he be delivered into the will of his adversaries (v 14).

The psalm ends as it began with an expression of serene confidence. The author has come through his tunnel of darkness. His faith has been sorely tried, but now it triumphs; *I am still confident of this: I will see the goodness of the LORD in the land of the living* (v 15). He who ardently desired to see with the eye of faith the beauty of the Lord (v 4) is sure that, before he dies, he will see the same Lord's goodness displayed in his own circumstances. So certain is he of this that he urges others to *wait for the* Lᴏʀᴅ (v 14), that is, to trust patiently in him. It is not enough to urge people to *be strong* and *take heart* (v 14). These would be empty sentiments unless they are both prefaced and followed by the other injunction to *wait for the* Lᴏʀᴅ. Courage can be no more than a Stoic virtue. It is only Christian when it is the fruit of a quiet confidence in God.

Psalm 29

The Voice of the Lord

A violent thunderstorm causes most people spasms of fear. Not so the Hebrew psalmist, who sees it rather as a manifestation of the glory of God. So convinced is he that God is in control of the elements, that he resorts to a bold anthropomorphism and calls the thunder *the voice of the LORD*. We must not imagine that he wants us to take him literally, any more than in other psalms, where the wind is his "breath", the heavens the work of his "fingers", and the animals feed from his open "hand" (see for example Psalms 147:18; 8:3 and 104:28). These are dramatic figures of speech for his immanent activity in the world.

¹Ascribe to the LORD, O mighty ones,
  ascribe to the LORD glory and strength.
²Ascribe to the LORD the glory due to his name;
  worship the LORD in the splendor of his holiness.
³The voice of the LORD is over the waters;
  the God of glory thunders,
  the LORD thunders over the mighty waters.
⁴The voice of the LORD is powerful;
  the voice of the LORD is majestic.
⁵The voice of the LORD breaks the cedars;
  the LORD breaks in pieces the cedars of Lebanon.
⁶He makes Lebanon skip like a calf,
  Sirion like a young wild ox.
⁷The voice of the LORD strikes with flashes of lightning.
⁸The voice of the LORD shakes the desert;
  The LORD shakes the Desert of Kadesh.
⁹The voice of the LORD twists the oaks
  and strips the forests bare.
And in his temple all cry, "Glory!"
¹⁰The LORD sits enthroned over the flood;
  the LORD is enthroned as King for ever.
¹¹The LORD gives strength to his people;
  the LORD blesses his people with peace.

The voice of the Lord

The poet seems to be describing the course of a thunderstorm as it comes from the north of Palestine (Lebanon and Sirion, or Mount Hermon, verses 5, 6) and passes overhead to vent its fury upon the *Desert of Kadesh* in the far south (v 8). Seven times *the voice of the LORD* is mentioned. One writer compares it to "successive peals of thunder," which reverberate over the countryside. At first it is heard *over the waters* (v 3), which seems to mean "above the rainclouds", *powerful and majestic* (v 4). But then the thunder comes closer, and the storm brings havoc in its train, breaking down the mighty *cedars of Lebanon*, and making the mountain itself shake till it seems to *skip like a calf...like a young wild ox* (v 6). The peals of thunder are accompanied by flashes of forked lightning (v 7). The deer give premature birth to their young (see margin), and the forests are stripped bare by the hurricane (v 9). So evident is the presence of God that the earth seems like his *temple.* Awestruck by his majesty, all cry *Glory!*

The glory of the Lord

This is one of several nature psalms. But it would be a grave mistake to suppose that the psalmist's intention is merely to give a poetic description of the beauties of nature. His world view is essentially God-centered. He is interested in sun and stars (Psalms 8, 19), thunder and lightning (Psalm 29), birds and beasts (Psalm 104), only because they speak to him of the greatness and the goodness of God. In Psalm 29 this is plain from the introduction and the conclusion.

The introduction (vs 1, 2) is a summons to the *mighty ones* to ascribe sovereignty to God. These "mighty ones" are angels, as is plain from Psalm 89:6 and Job 1:6; 2:1; 38:7. They *ascribe to the LORD the glory due to his name* (v 2). He is *the God of glory,* and his glory is partly manifest in the solemn magnificence of a thunderstorm.

If the introduction exhorts the angels in heaven to worship God, the conclusion is a prayer that this same God will bless his people on earth. His power to do so is undoubted, for he sits enthroned *over the flood* and reigns as *king for ever* (v 10). The transition from the description of the thunderstorm to the blessing of the people is important, because it shows that the Jews were aware of no dichotomy between nature and grace. The

God of the thunder was the God of Israel, sovereign over the elements as over the affairs of men and nations. The sanctuary was not only in Jerusalem, for the forest and the wilderness were his temple, in which he could be worshiped. A thunderstorm was not an alien phenomenon. Had not Jehovah revealed himself to his covenant people at Mount Sinai in thunder and lightning (Exodus 19:16; 20:18)? Yet he, whose voice is heard in the thunder, can also pacify the storm, making himself known in the still small voice as well as in the earthquake (1 Kings 19:11, 12). He is thus able to give to his people not only *strength* but *peace* (v 10).

Psalm 32

The Forgiveness and Guidance of God

The last two verses of this psalm form a good introduction to it. They contain the familiar, uncompromising biblical contrast between the *wicked* and the *righteous*, the believer and the unbeliever. The particular difference between these mentioned here is that, whereas *the woes of the wicked* are many, the righteous can *rejoice in the LORD and be glad*. It is further made clear that the ground of the joy of believers is that God's *unfailing love sur-*

¹Blessed is he
  whose transgressions are
    forgiven,
  whose sins are covered.
²Blessed is the man
  whose sin the LORD does not
    count against him
  and in whose spirit is no deceit.
³When I kept silent,
  my bones wasted away
    through my groaning all day
      long.
⁴For day and night
  your hand was heavy upon me;
my strength was sapped
  as in the heat of summer.
                    Selah
⁵Then I acknowledged my sin to
    you
  and did not cover up my
    iniquity.
I said, "I will confess
  my transgressions to the
    LORD"—
and you forgave
  the guilt of my sin.
                    Selah
⁶Therefore let everyone who is
  godly pray to you

while you may be found;
surely when the mighty waters
    rise,
  they will not reach him.
⁷You are my hiding place;
  you will protect me from
    trouble
  and surround me with songs
    of deliverance.
                    Selah
⁸I will instruct you and teach
  you in the way you should go;
  I will counsel you and watch
    over you.
⁹Do not be like the horse or the
    mule,
  which have no understanding
but must be controlled by bit
    and bridle
  or they will not come to you.
¹⁰Many are the woes of the
    wicked,
  but the LORD's unfailing love
  surrounds the man who trusts
    in him.
¹¹Rejoice in the LORD and be glad,
  you righteous;
  sing, all you who are upright
    in heart!

rounds them. Human joy arises from God's love, and the rest of the psalm unfolds its outworking in his forgiveness and guidance of the sinner.

God's forgiveness of the past (vs 1–8)

The psalm begins with two Old Testament beatitudes, affirming the blessedness not now of the person whose delight is in God's law (vs 1, 2), but of the person whose sins are forgiven. First, the facts of sin and forgiveness are described, in each case by three expressions. Wrong-doing is *transgression*, indicating a positive offence, a trespass, the stepping over a known boundary; and *sin*, a negative missing of the mark, an omission, the failure to attain an ideal; and "iniquity" (Revised Standard Version), that inward moral perversity or corruption of nature which we call "original sin".

Forgiveness is threefold too. The Hebrew word translated *forgiven* in verse 1 apparently means to remove or to lift. Sin is also *covered*, put out of sight; and therefore the Lord refuses to reckon it against the sinner. Forgiveness is thus regarded as the lifting of a burden, the covering of an ugly sight, and the canceling of a debt. It is these verses which the apostle Paul quoted in Romans 4:6–8 as an Old Testament example of God's justification of the sinner by his grace through faith, altogether apart from works.

From this general statement of the blessedness of being forgiven, David turns to a description from personal experience of the misery of refusing to confess sin. He has written of the person *in whose spirit is no deceit* (v 2), but now he depicts the painful consequences of deceit.

The reference is probably to his shameful dealings with Bathsheba, since, after committing adultery with her and murdering her husband, it was almost a year before he was brought to repentance by the ministry of the prophet Nathan (2 Samuel 11). During this period, while he tried to deceive himself and God, he had no peace. Indeed, long before the term "psychosomatic medicine" was coined, David tells how remorse and a tortured conscience resulted in alarming physical symptoms (vs 3, 4). But at last he gave in, acknowledged his sin to God and found peace through forgiveness (v 5).

David's vivid experience of forgiveness through repentance and confession leads him to urge others to do what he did and so receive what he received. Humble prayer to God, at a time when he may be found, always brings relief (v 6). Moreover, David resolves constantly to do the same himself (v 7). He has learned his lesson; he will not make the same mistake again.

God's guidance for the future (vs 8, 9)

David's expression of confidence in God to preserve him (v 8) is immediately answered. God gives him a promise of personal guidance, for in his steadfast love he is concerned not only to forgive the past but also to direct the future. God's guidance, like his forgiveness, is expressed in four verbs: *I will instruct you and teach you in the way you should go; I will counsel you and watch over you* (v 8). The picture seems to be of a mother teaching her child to walk. She never takes her eye off the child. Our God is just as tender and loving toward his people.

Nevertheless, it is important to see that verse 9 follows verse 8. God's promise of guidance is not intended to save us the bother of using our own intelligence. So to his promise he adds the command: *Do not be like the horse or the mule, which have no understanding but must be controlled by bit and bridle.* The sensitive horse and the stubborn mule have to be controlled and guided by pressure, even by force, because they are irrational animals. But we have been given a mind; we must not expect God to use a bit and bridle in his handling of us. He will treat us like human beings, not mules.

Blessed indeed are those who are surrounded by the steadfast love of God, forgiving their sins when they confess them to him, and guiding their footsteps when they trust his promises and obey his command to use their mind.

Psalm 34

Boasting in God

¹I will extol the Lord at all times;
  his praise will always be on my
  lips.
²My soul will boast in the Lord;
  let the afflicted hear and
  rejoice.
³Glorify the Lord with me;
  let us exalt his name together.
⁴I sought the Lord, and he
  answered me;
  he delivered me from all my
  fears.
⁵Those who look to him are
  radiant;
  their faces are never covered
  with shame.
⁶This poor man called, and the
  Lord heard him;
  he saved me out of all his
  troubles.
⁷The angel of the Lord encamps
  around those who fear him,
  and he delivers them.
⁸Taste and see that the Lord is
  good;
  blessed is the man who takes
  refuge in him.
⁹Fear the Lord, you his saints,
  for those who fear him lack
  nothing.
¹⁰The lions may grow weak and
  hungry,
  but those who seek the Lord
  lack no good thing.
¹¹Come, my children, listen to me;
  I will teach you the fear of the
  Lord.

¹²Whoever of you loves life
  and desires to see many good
  days,
¹³keep your tongue from evil
  and your lips from speaking
  lies.
¹⁴Turn from evil and do good;
  seek peace and pursue it.
¹⁵The eyes of the Lord are on the
  righteous
  and his ears are attentive to
  their cry;
¹⁶the face of the Lord is against
  those who do evil,
  to cut off the memory of them
  from the earth.
¹⁷The righteous cry out, and the
  Lord hears them;
  he delivers them from all their
  troubles.
¹⁸The Lord is close to the
  brokenhearted
  and saves those who are
  crushed in spirit.
¹⁹A righteous man may have many
  troubles,
  but the Lord delivers him from
  them all;
²⁰he protects all his bones,
  not one of them will be broken.
²¹Evil will slay the wicked;
  the foes of the righteous will
  be condemned.
²²The Lord redeems his servants;
  no-one who takes refuge in
  him will be condemned.

One of the notable features of this psalm is its combination of worship and witness. In answer to prayer the psalmist has been marvelously delivered by God from some great peril, and his gratitude brims over now in praise, now in exhortation to others to taste and see the Lord's goodness for themselves. He describes himself as "boasting in the LORD" (v 2). That is, he ascribes his salvation to the Lord, and because he does so out loud, those who hear him will give the glory to God too. C. H. Spurgeon, the great Baptist preacher, said: "The first ten verses are a hymn, and the last twelve a sermon."

A personal experience (vs 1–10)

The author is determined that his praise shall be no only a continuous (v 1) but congregational (vs 2, 3). Since it is *in the* LORD alone (emphatic) that his soul boasts, he knows that *the afflicted* will *hear and rejoice*, for this is the only kind of boasting which makes the humble glad. So he invites them to glorify the Lord with him (v 3), as later he urges them to look to the Lord themselves and become *radiant* (v 5).

The reason for his worship, and his summons to others to worship, is some particular and personal experience in which he cried to God and was delivered from all his fears (v 4) and all his troubles (v 6). He is evidently himself the *poor man* of verse 6. What the situation was out of which God delivered him the psalmist does not tell us.

Whatever the nature of the psalmist's distress, out of which he has been rescued, he is confident that God can do for others what he has done for him. *The angel of the* LORD (an Old Testament expression which often seems to indicate the presence of God himself) encircles those who fear him, as an army camps round a city to protect and deliver it (v 7). So sure of this is the psalmist, that he appeals to others to *taste and see* for themselves and to *fear the* LORD, since those who fear him *lack nothing* (vs 8, 9). Even the *lions*, singled out as "the strongest beasts of prey, most capable of providing for themselves", sometimes go hungry, but God's trusting people will *lack no good thing* (v 10).

The repeated references to "fear" in these verses are noteworthy. Deliverance from their fears (v 4) is promised to those who fear the Lord (vs 7, 9). This truth is neatly expressed in Tate and Brady's popular hymn paraphrasing this psalm, "Through All the Changing Scenes of Life":

> *Fear him, you saints, and you will then*
> *have nothing else to fear;*
> *his service shall be your delight,*
> *your needs shall be his care.*

To fear God is not, of course, to be frightened of him. Its meaning here is plain from its equivalents, namely, to "seek" him (v 4), to "call" to him (v 6) and "take refuge" in him (v 8), acknowledging our helplessness and looking to him for deliverance (compare Luke 1:50).

A general instruction (vs 11-22)

The psalmist's particular deliverance through the fear of the Lord leads him to a general instruction based upon his experience. Like the Preacher in the early chapters of the Book of Proverbs, he summons his pupils to gather round him, and chooses an appropriate theme (v 11). If they desire *many good days* (v 12), their fear of God must express itself not just in faith, but in works, that is, in moral behavior. No one can claim to fear God who does not depart from evil (compare Job 1:1; Proverbs 16:6) both in word (v 13) and in deed (v 14). Nor is it enough to turn away from evil; we must positively *do good* and patiently pursue peace (v 14).

Verses 15 to 18 describe the blessings which are granted to *the righteous*, that is, to those who fear God, shun evil, and do good. God's eyes and ears are directed toward them, while his face is turned away from the wicked (vs 15, 16). He hears and delivers the righteous, draws near to the *brokenhearted*, and saves the *crushed in spirit* (vs 17, 18).

This does not mean that the righteous are exempt from trouble. On the contrary, *a righteous man may have many troubles* (v 19). Nevertheless, God limits the afflictions of his people both in their duration and in their extent. He delivers them out of their trials (v 19) and, although they are often sorely wounded, he does not allow their bones to be broken (v 20), which seems to be a figure of speech for utter destruction (see also Micah 3:3). In Paul's language, "We are hard pressed on every side, but not crushed" (2 Corinthians 4:8).

To the unbeliever who asserts that this claim is contradicted in experience, we can only reply that, stated as a principle of God's surveillance over his people, it is true. Moreover, the differentiation between the fate of the wicked and the destiny of the righteous will finally be manifest by divine judgment in eternity. The wicked *will be condemned*; but *no-one who takes refuge in him will be condemned* (vs 21, 22).

Psalm 40

Out of the Horrible Pit

¹I waited patiently for the Lord;
　he turned to me and heard my
　　cry.
²He lifted me out of the slimy pit,
　out of the mud and mire;
he set my feet on a rock
　and gave me a firm place to
　　stand.
³He put a new song in my mouth,
　a hymn of praise to our God.
Many will see and fear
　and put their trust in the Lord.
⁴Blessed is the man
　who makes the Lord his trust,
who does not look to the proud,
　to those who turn aside to
　　false gods.
⁵Many, O Lord my God,
　are the wonders you have done.
The things you planned for us
　no-one can recount to you;
were I to speak and tell of them
　they would be too many to
　　declare.
⁶Sacrifice and offering you did not
　　desire,
　but my ears you have pierced;
burnt offerings and sin offerings
　you did not require.
⁷Then I said, "Here I am, I have
　　come—
　it is written about me in the
　　scroll.
⁸To do your will, O my God, is my
　　desire;
　your law is within my heart."
⁹I proclaim righteousness in the
　　great assembly;
　I do not seal my lips,
as you know, O Lord.
¹⁰I do not hide your
　righteousness in my heart;
I speak of your faithfulness
　and salvation.
I do not conceal your love and
　your truth
　from the great assembly.
¹¹Do not withhold your mercy
　from me, O Lord;
may your love and your truth
　always protect me.
¹²For troubles without number
　surround me;
my sins have overtaken me,
　and I cannot see.
They are more than the hairs of
　my head,
and my heart fails within me.
¹³Be pleased, O Lord, to save me;
　O Lord, come quickly to help
　　me.
¹⁴May all who seek to take my life
　be put to shame and confusion;
may all who desire my ruin
　be turned back in disgrace.
¹⁵May those who say to me, "Aha!
　Aha!"
be appalled at their own shame.
¹⁶But may all who seek you
　rejoice and be glad in you;
may those who love your
　salvation always say,
　"The Lord be exalted!"
¹⁷Yet I am poor and needy;
　may the Lord think of me.
You are my help and my deliverer;
　O my God, do not delay.

Every Christian believer is fortified in present trial by the memory of past blessings. Because we have experienced God's faithfulness in former days we are encouraged to trust him still. Such is the theme of this psalm, which begins with a graphic description of deliverance and ends with an urgent plea for continued mercy.

An account of past deliverance (vs 1-10)

The psalmist was down a *slimy pit*, full of *mud and mire*. There is no need to suppose that this was literally his plight, like Jeremiah, whose enemies let him down by ropes into a cistern until he sank into the slime (Jeremiah 38:1-13). The pit and the bog no doubt symbolize some desolate experience of sin or depression or disease. In his helplessness, unable himself to climb out, he *waited patiently for the LORD*, and the following verses emphasize, stage by stage, the mighty deliverance of God who first heard his cry, then stooped down and drew him out of the mud, then set his feet securely upon rock, and finally put a fresh song of praise in his mouth, leading many to believe (vs 1-3).

Such an experience of salvation has several fruitful consequences, notably worship (vs 4-6), obedience (vs 7-9), and witness (vs 10-12). His worship is expressed both in exclaiming how blessed the believer is (v 4) and how numberless are the deeds and thoughts of God (v 5).

But true worship goes beyond verbal exclamations. It is more even than the offering of sacrifices. It involves the offering of ourselves in a life of moral obedience. (For the precedence of obedience over sacrifice see 1 Samuel 15:22; Isaiah 1:10-17; Jeremiah 7:21-26; Hosea 6:6; Micah 6:6-8). This obedience is demanded *in the scroll*, that is, the written law. It begins in our *ears*, which God has *pierced*, or literally (v 6) "dug", so that he has enabled us to hear and grasp his will.

But God in grace does more even than this. If he has written his law in a book, that we may know it, and whispered it into our ears, that we may understand it, he also inscribes it in our hearts, so that we "delight to do it" (v 8, Revised Standard Version). This statement of knowing, loving and doing God's will, which is partially true of all his children, found its perfect fulfilment in his incarnate Son, to whom it is applied in Hebrews 10:5-9.

Salvation provokes within us, however, more than a

Godward response of spiritual worship and moral obedience; it teaches us also to care for our fellows, that they too may hear of God's grace. So the psalmist asserts repeatedly that he has not concealed God's *love and...truth* (that is, faithfulness) *from the great assembly* but has publicly declared it (vs 9–10). When God sets our feet on the rock and puts his law in our ears and in our hearts, we cannot keep our lips from making his goodness known.

A prayer for present help (vs 11–17)

As in Psalm 27, the mood changes abruptly in the middle from affirmation to supplication, from a rehearsal of God's *love and...truth* to a plea that they will always preserve him. For again the psalmist finds himself in peril and distress. *Troubles without number* have encompassed him, and this time he does not leave us in ignorance of their nature: *my sins have overtaken me and I cannot see.* Indeed, they are not only too strong for him to conquer, but too many for him to count. His heart fails him (v 12), and in self-despair he cries to God to deliver him (v 13).

The psalm ends with a contrast between two different kinds of "seeker", those who *seek to take my life* and those *who seek you*, in a word, the godly and the ungodly. The ungodly betray their ungodliness in their persecution of the godly, and three times the psalmist prays for their overthrow (vs 14, 15). But for those who instead seek God and love his salvation he desires a different destiny, namely that they may have cause from their experience to say continually, *"The LORD be exalted!"* (v 16). Among such he numbers himself. Left to himself, he knows he is *poor and needy*, but the Lord, who has been his deliverer, cares for him still and will yet deliver him again (v 17).

Psalms 42, 43

The Causes and Cure of Spiritual Depression

The subject of this psalm (for Psalms 42 and 43 seem clearly to belong together) is spiritual depression, its causes and cure. The author's soul is *downcast* (v 5), and *disturbed* within him. This is an experience by no means rare, even among godly people. Christian biographies supply many examples. Moreover, it is almost certain that our Lord himself was alluding to these verses when he cried both "Now my heart is troubled" and "My soul is overwhelmed with sorrow" (John 12:27; Mark 14:34).

Psalm 42

¹As the deer pants for streams of water,
so my soul pants for you, O God.
²My soul thirsts for God, for the living God.
When can I go and meet God?
³My tears have been my food day and night,
while men say to me all day long,
"Where is your God?"
⁴These things I remember as I pour out my soul:
how I used to go with the multitude,
leading the procession to the house of God,
with shouts of joy and thanksgiving among the festive throng.
⁵Why are you downcast, O my soul?
Why so disturbed within me?
Put your hope in God,
for I will yet praise him,
my Savior and ⁶my God.

My soul is downcast within me;
therefore I will remember you from the land of the Jordan,
the heights of Hermon—from Mount Mizar.
⁷Deep calls to deep in the roar of your waterfalls;
all your waves and breakers have swept over me.
⁸By the day the LORD directs his love,
at night his song is with me—
a prayer to the God of my life.
⁹I say to God my Rock,
"Why have you forgotten me?
Why must I go about mourning, oppressed by the enemy?"
¹⁰My bones suffer mortal agony as my foes taunt me,
saying to me all day long,
"Where is your God?"
¹¹Why are you downcast, O my soul?
Why so disturbed within me?
Put your hope in God,
for I will yet praise him,
my Savior and my God.

Psalm 43

¹Vindicate me, O God,
  and plead my cause against an
    ungodly nation;
  rescue me from deceitful and
    wicked men.
²You are God my stronghold.
  Why have you rejected me?
Why must I go about mourning,
  oppressed by the enemy?
³Send forth your light and your
    truth,
  let them guide me;

let them bring me to your holy
    mountain,
  to the place where you dwell.
⁴Then will I go to the altar of God,
  to God, my joy and my delight.
I will praise you with the harp,
  O God, my God.
⁵Why are you downcast, O my
    soul?
  Why so disturbed within me?
Put your hope in God,
  for I will yet praise him,
    my Savior and my God.

What is particularly moving is that the psalmist does not acquiesce in his condition, but three times, in words which form a refrain, he questions himself about his despondency and summons himself to trust in God (42:6, 7, 14, 15 and 43:5, 6).

So the psalm forms three stanzas. Each begins with the psalmist's grief, in which he addresses God or his readers, and ends with the refrain, in which he addresses himself.

The causes of spiritual depression

At first the author portrays himself not as cast down, but as thirsty. He thirsts for God, as a *deer* thirsts for water when overtaken by hunters or by drought. In C. S. Lewis's phrase, he has a keen "appetite for God". This is natural and right. It is, or should be, the experience of every believer. Though indeed God "satisfies the thirsty and fills the hungry with good things" (Psalm 107:9; compare Psalm 36:8, 9), yet our hunger and thirst for him are satisfied only to break out again more fiercely (compare Psalm 63:1, 2).

In this case, however, the author's thirst is aggravated by two factors, which he immediately mentions. The first is expressed in the form of a question: *When can I go and meet with God?* (v 2). This is what the Israelite was required to do three times a year, visiting Jerusalem for the major festivals (see Exodus 23:17), and this evidently the psalmist was unable to do. Secondly, his daily diet was one of tears because men were constantly taunting him: *Where is your God?* (v 3). These, then, were the causes of his depression of soul: the absence of God to comfort him and the presence of men who mocked him. Each stanza reverts to this double theme.

His sense of estrangement from God is due to his enforced separation from the Temple and its worship. He writes from northern Palestine. *Mount Mizar* (v 6) has not been identified, but is evidently a hill in the Hermon range. From this distant hill he thinks of God's *holy mountain* (43:3) and longs to be there again. Wistfully he remembers the sheer joy of worship in former days (v 4).

As Psalm 42 is entitled *"A Maskil* (meaning perhaps 'an instruction') *of the Sons of Korah"*, it has been suggested that the author may have been one of the Korahites, men descended from Korah (Levi's great-grandson), who were gatekeepers, watchers, and musicians in the Temple (1 Chronicles 6:22–48; 9:17–32; 2 Chronicles 20:19). Certainly he writes here of praising the Lord with his voice and his harp (42:11; 43:4). But he cannot do so now because he is in exile. Instead of the Temple music he is deafened by the thunder of waterfalls and of mountain torrents in spate, as *deep calls to deep*, echoing across the valley. They seem to symbolize his calamities; he calls them God's *waves and breakers*, which have *swept over* him (v 7). He longs to take part again in the Temple worship by day and by night (v 9).

So, in the third stanza, he prays that God will send out his light and his truth, which like guides in the desert will lead him safely back to God's hill, dwelling, and altar, so that there again he may encounter and worship the God of his joy and gladness (43:3, 4). These sentiments need not be pressed into meaning that he supposed the Temple to be the only meeting place of the soul with God—for much of the psalm is itself addressed to God while he is in exile; what he ardently desires is a renewal of that special communion with God which he had experienced in public worship on the great festivals.

The second cause of his depression is the scoffing of the heathen who kept asking incredulously: *Where is your God?* (vs 3, 10). It is partly that they were idolaters, serving gods they could see and touch, while *the living God* was invisible (v 2, compare Psalm 115:2); and partly that God appeared as inactive as he was invisible, and did not immediately vindicate his people when they were oppressed by their enemies (compare Psalm 79:10). The psalmist feels forgotten (v 9). His spirit is so sensitive that the sharp pain of the scoffers' taunts seems like a mortal wound in his body (v 10). He prays for vindication and deliverance (43:1).

It is, then, this combination of circumstances which has brought the psalmist to depression, and even to despair: people ridicule him for his faith in the living God, while the living God whom they mock seems indifferent and far away.

The cure for spiritual depression

Each stanza, in which the author describes his sorrowful plight, concludes with the same splendid refrain (42:5, 11; 43:5). It is remarkable to note how the author speaks to himself. He will not give in to his moods. He takes himself in hand and reproaches himself for his depression. He recognizes that his soul is weighed down as by a crushing burden, and inwardly *disturbed* like the raging of the sea (Psalm 46:3). But why? he asks himself. Within his repeated self-questioning is an implied rebuke. Instead of answering his own questions, or excusing himself, he immediately prescribes his remedy: he must trust or "hope" in God. He must give up his introspection and self-pity, his wistful reminiscences and his pained resentment at the mockery of his enemies.

The cure for depression is neither to look in at our grief, nor back to our past, nor round at our problems, but away and up to the living God. He is our help and our God, and if we trust him now, we shall soon have cause to praise him again. Thus, as one writer sums up, "faith rebukes despondency and hope triumphs over despair".

Why restless, why cast down, my soul?
Hope still, and you shall sing
The praise of him who is your God,
Your health's eternal spring.

(Tate and Brady, 1696)

Psalm 46

Immanuel, God With Us

The name of Martin Luther will always be associated with this psalm. His famous hymn *"Ein' feste Burg ist unser Gott"* is a free paraphrase of it. He and Philip Melanchthon would sing it together in times of dark discouragement, and Thomas Carlyle has made it familiar to English readers by his translation "A Safe Stronghold our God is still." It is a sublime expression of quiet confidence in God's sovereignty amid the upheavals of nature and history.

The original context was evidently some notable deliverance of Jerusalem from the attack of heathen invaders. *The city of God* (v 4) was favored with several such deliverances. But the situation envisaged in the psalm, together with its resemblance in metaphor and phrase to some of Isaiah's prophecies, suggest the overthrow of Sennacherib's army in 701 B.C..

¹God is our refuge and strength,
  an ever present help in trouble.
²Therefore we will not fear,
    though the earth give way
  and the mountains fall into the
    heart of the sea,
³though its waters roar and foam
  and the mountains quake with
    their surging.
        Selah
⁴There is a river whose streams
    make glad the city of God,
  the holy place where the Most
    High dwells.
⁵God is within her, she will not
    fall;
  God will help her at break of
    day.
⁶Nations are in uproar, kingdoms
    fall;

he lifts his voice, the earth
    melts.
⁷The Lᴏʀᴅ Almighty is with us;
  the God of Jacob is our fortress.
        Selah
⁸Come and see the works of the
    Lᴏʀᴅ,
  the desolations he has brought
    on the earth.
⁹He makes wars cease to the ends
    of the earth;
  he breaks the bow and shatters
    the spear,
  he burns the shields with fire.
¹⁰Be still, and know that I am God;
  I will be exalted among the
    nations,
  I will be exalted in the earth."
¹¹The Lᴏʀᴅ Almighty is with us;
  the God of Jacob is our fortress.
        Selah

Although Hezekiah was King of Judah, he was a vassal of Sennacherib and was obliged to pay tribute to him. When he rebelled, the mighty army of the Assyrians came sweeping west and south like the irresistible waves of the sea. Jerusalem was soon surrounded. Sennacherib boasted that he had shut up Hezekiah "like a caged bird" and demanded his surrender.

The situation was critical. Twenty years previously Sennacherib's predecessor had taken by storm the northern capital of Samaria and depopulated the land of Israel. It looked as if Judah was to suffer the same fate. Hezekiah appealed to the prophet Isaiah, who spoke to him the word of the Lord: "Do not be afraid...for I will defend this city to save it." Suddenly and dramatically, as the secular historian Herodotus bore witness, God intervened. "That night the angel of the Lord went out and put to death 185,000 men in the Assyrian camp. When the people got up early the next morning—there were all the dead bodies!" So Sennacherib withdrew. (See 2 Kings 18 and 19.)

The psalm is in three parts, expressing first a general confidence in the power and providence of God, then a particular experience of it in the deliverance of the city, and lastly an assurance that he will establish his universal kingdom of peace. The second and third stanzas are followed by the refrain: *The Lord Almighty is with us; the God of Jacob is our fortress* (vs 7, 11). The demands of symmetry suggest that the same refrain originally concluded the first stanza also. It is not only a statement of God's protection, but that he who is our fortress is both the powerful *Lord Almighty* and the faithful *God of Jacob*, who is bound to his people in a solemn covenant.

A general confidence (vs 1-3)

The psalmist affirms that *God is our refuge and strength and an ever present help in trouble.* It is this confidence which enables him to add almost with defiance: *Therefore we will not fear.* Even the worst convulsions of nature—earthquake, storm, and tempest—which strike terror into the hearts of defenseless people, will not make us afraid (vs 2, 3).

A special experience (vs 4-7)

In contrast to the sea whose waters *roar and foam* (v 3), the psalmist now mentions other and calmer waters, those of *a river whose streams make glad the city of God* (v 4). The original reference must be to the waters of Siloam, whose gentle flowing Isaiah used as a picture of the quiet, beneficent providence of God (Isaiah 8:6). The symbol reappears in the visions of both Ezekiel (Ezekiel 47:1–12) and John (Revelation 22:1–5).

Under God's gracious rule his city is made glad (v 4) and simply cannot *fall* because *God is within her* to protect and help her (v 5). Let the nations "roar" like the sea and kingdoms "quake" like mountains (the same verbs are used in verse 6 as in verses 2 and 3), yet God has only to speak and *the earth melts* before him. That is, before the voice of the Lord, the Assyrian army was scattered.

A final assurance (vs 8–11)

The writer now summons the people to take note of God's decisive intervention in the protection of Jerusalem and the *desolation* of her foes (v 8). This divine deliverance is seen as a pledge and foretaste of the day when God will finally overthrow all warmongers and establish his kingdom of peace; *he breaks the bow and shatters the spear, he burns the shields with fire* (v 9). The vision recalls the prophecies of Isaiah about the beating of spears into plowshares and spears into pruninghooks, and the using of military boots and bloodstained garments as fuel for the fire (Isaiah 2:4; 9:5).

No sooner has this promise of peace been given than God himself, its guarantor, is heard to speak: *Be still, and know that I am God.* It was his voice which overthrew the Assyrians (v 6); it is his voice which pacifies his people. He is God for ever and is already here and now (probably a present tense) exalted in the earth (v 10). This majestic affirmation prompts his people to respond in the refrain: *The Lord Almighty is with us.* Again, the words have an Isaianic ring, reminding us of his great prophecy about Immanuel, "God with us" (Isaiah 7:14; 8:8, 10).

We also live in an epoch of crisis. The old order has gone. The social revolution begun 150 years ago continues and grows in pace. We hear wars and rumors of wars. People's hearts fail them for fear. Can we say: "We will not fear"? Indeed we can; but only if we believe the other affirmations of this psalm: *I am God* and *The Lord Almighty is with us.* As John Wesley said with his dying breath: "The best of all is, God is with us."

Psalm 51

Divine Mercy for the Penitent

[1]Have mercy on me, O God,
according to your unfailing
love;
according to your great
compassion
blot out my transgressions.
[2]Wash away all my iniquity
and cleanse me from my sin.
[3]For I know my transgressions,
and my sin is always before me.
[4]Against you, you only, have I
sinned
and done what is evil in your
sight,
so that you are proved right when
you speak
and justified when you judge.
[5]Surely I have been a sinner from
birth,
sinful from the time my mother
conceived me.
[6]Surely you desire truth in the
inner parts;
you teach me wisdom in the
inmost place.
[7]Cleanse me with hyssop, and I
shall be clean;
wash me, and I shall be whiter
than snow.
[8]Let me hear joy and gladness;
let the bones you have
crushed rejoice.
[9]Hide your face from my sins
and blot out all my iniquity.
[10]Create in me a pure heart, O
God,
and renew a steadfast spirit
within me.

[11]Do not cast me from your
presence
or take your Holy Spirit from
me.
[12]Restore to me the joy of your
salvation
and grant me a willing spirit,
to sustain me.
[13]Then I will teach transgressors
your ways,
and sinners will turn back to
you.
[14]Save me from bloodguiltiness,
O God,
the God who saves me,
and my tongue will sing of
your righteousness.
[15]O Lord, open my lips,
and my mouth will declare your
praise.
[16]You do not delight in sacrifice,
or I would bring it;
you do not take pleasure in
burnt offerings.
[17]The sacrifices of God are a
broken spirit;
a broken and contrite heart,
O God, you will not despise.
[18]In your good pleasure make Zion
prosper;
build up the walls of Jerusalem.
[19]Then there will be righteous
sacrifices,
whole burnt offerings to
delight you;
then bulls will be offered on
your altar.

Psalm 46 sets forth the sovereignty of God; this psalm extols his mercy. Though he is exalted among the nations (Psalm 46:10), he does not despise the broken and contrite heart of the penitent (51:17).

This fourth of the seven so-called "penitential psalms" refers in its title to David's grievous sin. From his palace roof one spring afternoon, he saw a beautiful woman named Bathsheba, desired her for himself, and committed adultery with her. He had her husband, Uriah the Hittite, sent into the hottest part of the battle with the Ammonites, where he would certainly be killed and, in fact, was killed. David then proceeded to take her as his wife. Only when the prophet Nathan was sent by God to rebuke him, did he feel his guilt, confess his sin, and plead for mercy. His simple "I have sinned against the LORD" in 2 Samuel 12:13 is here elaborated into such a prayer for God's mercy in cleansing and renewal as has been the language of penitents ever since.

The need of God's mercy

We can appreciate our need of divine mercy only when we have seen the gravity of our sin. As in Psalm 32, so in verses 1 and 2 of this psalm, three separate Hebrew words are used to describe David's offense, namely *transgression* (the crossing of a boundary), *sin* (the missing of a mark), and *iniquity* (depravity of nature). The thought behind these words is unfolded in an important recognition of the essence and origin of sin.

The essence of sin is revolt against against God: *Against you, you only, have I sinned and done what is evil in your sight, so that you are proved right when you speak and justified when you judge* (v 4). It is true that David had sinned against Bathsheba and Uriah, against his family and nation, but first and foremost, he had offended against the love and law of God. He had coveted, stolen, committed adultery and murder and, in so doing, had broken four of the five last commandments and brought himself under the just sentence of God. Compare Romans 3:4 where Paul quotes these words to establish the unswerving justice of God in his dealings with human beings. It is because we are under the judgment of God that we need the mercy of God.

If the essence of sin is rebellion, its origin is in our fallen nature: *Surely I was sinful at birth, sinful from the time my mother conceived me* (v 5). This does not, of course, mean that the marvelous processes of conception and birth are in themselves sinful, but that our human nature from its first beginnings has been infected with sin. As we inherit it from our parents, it is twisted with self-centeredness. This is "original sin", and David came to recognize it when his sinful passions of lust, jealousy, cruelty, and avarice overcame and overthrew him.

It is when we see ourselves as we are, on the one hand rebels against God and under the judgment of God, and on the other prisoners of a corrupt nature, that we come, like David, to despair of ourselves and to cry to God for mercy.

The expression of God's mercy

The mercy of God expresses itself in meeting the sinner's need, giving him both pardon and purity.

In praying for pardon, David uses two vivid metaphors. First, he asks God to *blot out* his transgressions (vs 1, 9). The verb denotes the removal of writing from a book (see for example Exodus 32:32). He seems to think of his sins as a list of offenses of which he is accused or a catalogue of debts which he cannot pay. He pleads that the entry be erased.

Secondly, he acknowledges that his sins have defiled him and prays that God will *wash* and *cleanse* him (v 2), until his black stains are removed and he becomes *whiter than snow* (v 7). Since in certain Old Testament rituals a bunch of hyssop was dipped in blood or water, which was then ceremonially sprinkled, the word *hyssop* is used in verse 7 as a symbol of cleansing.

But David knew his need of purity as well as pardon. God demanded *truth in the inner parts* (v 6); yet David's very nature was corrupt (v 5). Only the creative power of God could make him a new person. So he prayed: *Create in me a pure heart, O God, and renew a steadfast spirit within me* (v 10). He longed, that is, for a new nature with new and pure desires, and for a spirit both *steadfast* (v 10) and *willing* (v 12). He seems to have known too, before the full New Testament revelation had been given, that such a new nature and spirit could be imparted to him only by the Holy Spirit himself (v 12).

If God in mercy would grant him both a clean conscience and a clean heart, the sorrow which his sin had caused would be turned into *joy and gladness* (v 8, compare v 12).

The results of God's mercy

The last part of the psalm (vs 13–19) is devoted to the results which follow an experience of the cleansing and recreating mercy of God. David resolves that his attitude both to other people and to God will be different.

First, he accepts his responsibility to his fellow humans. He has sinned against them; now he will serve them in a new way. When his own transgressions have been forgiven, he will *teach transgressors* God's way, so that they return to him (v 13). He prays to be delivered from *bloodguilt* (v 14). Perhaps he means that, although he has indeed been guilty of the blood of Uriah, he is determined that God shall not require at his hand the blood of sinners whom he has failed to warn and teach (compare Ezekiel 3:16–27 and 33:1–20).

His second responsibility is toward God. He will use his lips in worship as well as witness: *O Lord, open my lips, and my mouth will declare your praise* (v 15). It is this that God desires, not *sacrifice* or *burnt offerings*. He does not mean that no sacrifice at all is pleasing to God, but that the kind of sacrifice he chiefly desires, especially from a transgressor like David, is *a broken and contrite heart*. And then, when he is forgiven, he may offer the further sacrifice of praise and thanksgiving (v 15; compare Psalm 50:14, 23).

The last two verses have seemed to many commentators not to belong to David's psalm at all. There is an apparent reference to the rebuilding of Jerusalem's walls in verse 18, although the words could be figurative. And verse 19 (*burnt offerings to delight you*) seems to contradict verse 16 (*you do not take pleasure in burnt offerings*). The discrepancy is only superficial, however, and is consistent with much teaching in both psalms and prophets. This is not that sacrifices are not acceptable to God in themselves, but that they please him only if they are expressive of a contrite, worshiping heart and an obedient will.

Psalm 67

Saving Health to the Nations

This psalm appears to be greatly concerned about the blessing of God. Three times in its brief seven verses it reverts to this theme, now in prayer that God may bless us, and now in affirmation that he will do so.

This gives the psalm a rather homely touch, because we ourselves frequently talk about the blessing of God. "God bless you," we say as we bid someone goodbye, or as we end a letter. We even utter the same prayer when people sneeze! We seem so anxious to secure the divine blessing for our friends, that we lose no opportunity of expressing our desire for it.

Now what do we mean when we seek God's blessing? The language of this psalm is rather beautiful because it is borrowed from the words of the high priest's blessing. First given by God to Moses, for use by Aaron and his sons in the Tabernacle worship, it is recorded in Numbers 6:24–26, "The LORD bless you and keep you; the LORD make his face to shine upon you and be gracious to you; the LORD turn his face towards you and give you peace." This blessing came to be used regularly in the Temple services at Jerusalem, and is still a favorite in Christian worship

¹May God be gracious to us and
   bless us
 and make his face to shine
   upon us;
              Selah
²may your ways be known on
   earth,
 your salvation among all
   nations.
³May the peoples praise you,
   O God;
 may all the peoples praise you.
⁴May the nations be glad and
   sing for joy,

for you rule the peoples justly
 and guide the nations of the
   earth.
              Selah
⁵May the peoples praise you,
   O God;
 may all the peoples praise you.
⁶Then the land will yield its
   harvest,
 and God, our God, will bless us.
⁷God will bless us,
 and all the ends of the earth
   will fear him.

today. Echoes of it are heard in several psalms (for instance Psalm 4:6; 29:11; 31:16; 80:3, 7, 55). So here some words from the ancient blessing of Aaron form the groundwork of this psalm, which was no doubt composed for liturgical use in the Temple.

When we read as a whole, Psalm 67 teaches us that there is some justification for praying for ourselves, that there are unselfish reasons for praying the selfish prayer *God bless us*. Two such motives are given—immediate and ultimate.

The knowledge of God

The first reason why we desire that God shall bless us in order that through us his salvation may be known to all humankind (vs 1, 2). In that case Israel's motive in seeking God's blessing was not selfish after all. They prayed that God would bless them, not in order to wallow comfortably in his blessing themselves, but in order that it might pass from them to others. They longed that God would be merciful to them, that thereby the nations might receive his mercy, and come to know his ways and saving health.

We need to remember that Israel made very audacious claims for herself and her God. She claimed to be the special people of God, with whom he had entered into an everlasting covenant. She poked fun at the dead, dumb idols of the nations. She affirmed that her God was the only living, active, and true God. So of course her heathen neighbors were watching her, now quizzically, now incredulously. They wanted some evidence to support Israel's contention. "Where is now your God?" they asked. They wanted to know what God could do for his people; what difference he made to them; whether the claims of Israel had any substance to them.

That is why Israel prayed *God be gracious to us and bless us*. If only Aaron's blessing would come true! If only God's mercy were granted to them! If only God were specially to bless them, and the light of his smile were to be upon them and with them always! Surely then the nations would see for themselves? Then the nations would have visual proof of the existence, activity, and grace of God? Then the nations would come to know his way and his salvation, and experience themselves that God rules righteously and leads his people like a shepherd (v 4).

The same principle operates today. Non-Christian people are watching us. We claim to know, to love, and to follow Jesus

Christ. We say that he is our Savior, our Lord, and our Friend. "What difference does he make to these Christians?" the world asks searchingly. "Where is their God?" It may be said without fear of contradiction that the greatest hindrance to evangelism in the world today is the failure of the church to supply evidence in her own life and work of the saving power of God. Rightly may we pray for ourselves that we may have God's blessing and mercy and the light of his countenance—not that we may then monopolize his grace and bask in the sunshine of his favor, but that others may see in us his blessing and his beauty, and be drawn to him through us.

The worship of God

Verses 3–5 form another refrain in this psalm. They give the second reason why we desire God's blessing. It is not just in order that others may come to know him. For why do we want them to know God? Just for their own benefit? Just that they may receive his salvation? Are we wanting others to do what we have renounced ourselves? We are not asking God's blessing for our selfish ends; are we content that others should receive his blessing for theirs? That hardly makes sense.

We need to look beyond the salvation of the nations to its ultimate purpose, which is that they too should come to worship and praise God. We should desire their salvation not just that they shall know him for themselves, but that they shall praise him for himself. The greatest incentive in all evangelism is not the need of human beings but the glory of God; not that they shall receive salvation, but that they shall give to God the honor that is due to his name, acknowledging and adoring him for ever. We cannot be content until every convert has become a worshiper.

Psalm 73

The Prosperity of the Wicked

¹Surely God is good to Israel,
  to those who are pure in heart.
²But as for me, my feet had
    almost slipped;
  I had nearly lost my foothold.
³For I envied the arrogant
  when I saw the prosperity of
    the wicked.
⁴They have no struggles;
  their bodies are healthy and
    strong.
⁵They are free from the burdens
    common to man;
  they are not plagued by human
    ills.
⁶Therefore pride is their necklace;
  they clothe themselves with
    violence.
⁷From their callous hearts comes
    iniquity;
  the evil conceits of their
    minds know no limits.
⁸They scoff, and speak with
    malice;
  in their arrogance they
    threaten oppression.
⁹Their mouths lay claim to heaven,
  and their tongues take
    possession of the earth.
¹⁰Therefore their people turn to
    them
  and drink up waters in
    abundance.
¹¹They say, "How can God know?
  Does the Most High have
    knowledge?"
¹²This is what the wicked are like—
  always carefree, they increase
    in wealth.
¹³Surely in vain have I kept my
    heart pure;
  in vain have I washed my hands
    in innocence.
¹⁴All day long I have been plagued;
  I have been punished every
    morning.
¹⁵If I had said, "I will speak thus,"
  I would have betrayed your
    children.
¹⁶When I tried to understand all
    this,
  it was oppressive to me
¹⁷till I entered the sanctuary of
    God;
  then I understood their final
    destiny.
¹⁸Surely you place them on
    slippery ground;
  you cast them down to ruin.
¹⁹How suddenly are they
    destroyed,
  completely swept away by
    terrors!
²⁰As a dream when one awakes,
  so when you arise, O LORD,
  you will despise them as
    fantasies.
²¹When my heart was grieved
  and my spirit embittered,
²²I was senseless and ignorant;
  I was a brute beast before you.
²³Yet I am always with you;
  you hold me by my right hand.
²⁴You guide me with your counsel,
  and afterwards you will take
    me into glory.

> ²⁵Whom have I in heaven but you?
>   And earth has nothing I desire
>   besides you.
> ²⁶My flesh and my heart may fail,
>   but God is the strength of my
>   heart
>   and my portion for ever.
> ²⁷Those who are far from you will
>   perish;
> you destroy all who are
>   unfaithful to you.
> ²⁸But as for me, it is good to be
>   near God.
> I have made the Sovereign
>   Lord my refuge;
> I will tell of all your deeds.

The providence of God, his moral ordering of the world, is a problem which has always baffled the human mind. The book of Job and Psalms 37 and 49 as well as 73 are devoted to this theme. The problem can be simply stated. God has revealed himself as good and just, punishing wickedness and rewarding goodness. If he is all-powerful as well as all-good, why does he allow such a morally perverse state of affairs to continue on earth? Far from justice catching up on the wicked, they flourish "like a green tree" (Psalm 37:35). They not only get away with their wickedness but seem to be exempt from the troubles which befall other people. In a word, honesty is not the best policy. It does not pay to be good. It is the wicked who prosper, while adversity overtakes the righteous. Such is the background to this psalm.

The problem (vs 1–14)

The psalmist begins with the conviction held by all godly people, even in the face of apparently contradictory circumstances: *Surely God is good…to those who are pure in heart* (v 1). This is an axiom of revealed religion and cannot on any account be surrendered. *But as for me*, he immediately continues, *my feet had almost slipped; I had nearly lost my foothold. For I envied* the arrogant when I saw the prosperity of the wicked (vs 2, 3). First, he was troubled by their immunity to disease and disaster (vs 4, 5). Next, by their arrogance (vs 6–9). Their eyes and heart, their talk and looks (vs 7, 8) are full of conceit. Not only do *their tongues take possession of the earth* (v 9), but they even *lay claim to heaven* (v 9). Added to their immunity to trouble and their arrogant ways is their popularity with the world (vs 10, 11). The people ask why God, if indeed he knows about them, does not punish them (v 11).

The psalmist concludes his description of the wicked: *always carefree, they increase in wealth.* Then he cries out bitterly: *Surely in vain have I kept my heart pure* (v 13), for while the wicked flourish, *all day long I have been plagued* (v 14). If the wicked prosper, it is vain to be righteous. Righteousness does not pay; the big dividends go to the wicked.

The right approach to the problem (vs 15, 16)

The reason why the psalmist so nearly stumbled and fell (v 2) is that his approach was wrong. He made at least three mistakes. First, he *envied* the wicked (v 3). But it is always wrong to envy the sinner's liberty to sin. "Do not let your heart envy sinners, but always be zealous for the fear of the LORD" (Proverbs 23:17). Secondly, he became bitter against God, as he later confesses (vs 21–22). To make presumptuous complaints against God is to behave like an ignorant animal, not like a rational human being. Thirdly, he was tempted to give up. When he tried to understand, he says, *it was oppressive to me* (v 16). He could find no solution and was inclined to give in to despair.

But perplexity and hopelessness lasted only *till I entered the sanctuary of God* (v 17). Perception is granted to those who humbly seek God's face. The Christian in the twentieth century needs to learn this lesson. When we are perplexed by the problems of God's providential rule in the world, we are neither to look at the wicked with envy nor at ourselves in bitter self-pity. Nor should we give up looking for any solution and lapse into despair, but rather fall on our knees and look at God. Then "from the secret place of the Most High we see things as God sees them" (Campbell Morgan).

The solution (vs 17–27)

Our problems are aggravated because we are narrow-minded and short-sighted. It is a question of perspective. A mountain which appears menacing when we stand at its foot and it towers above us, shrinks into harmless insignificance when we view it from a distance or from the air. So the problem of God's providence cannot be solved in the limited context of time and earth; its solution awaits the next world and eternity. Many of life's inequalities will remain now. But wrongs will be righted, evil avenged, and good vindicated in the final judgment. This is why we need to keep going into *the sanctuary of God*; it is there that our perspective is adjusted and our vision clarified.

What the psalmist was able in God's sanctuary to grasp was the *final destiny* of these people (v 17). They flourish now, it is true, but God sets them *on slippery ground*. In the words of Jesus, they are on "the broad road that leads to destruction". Ultimately death will claim them and they will be *destroyed*. Indeed, *as a dream when one awakes*, the very memory of them will vanish away (vs 17–19).

If that is the fate of the wicked, very different is the destiny of the righteous: *I am always with you* (v 23). That is, though the ungodly flourish now, only to perish in the end, the godly enjoy the presence of God perpetually, both now and forever (v 24). God's people may suffer want and persecution, but their abiding wealth is in God himself. In one of the sublimest expressions of personal religion in the Old Testament the psalmist continues: *Whom have I in heaven but you? And earth has nothing I desire besides you* (v 25). In heaven and earth, in time and eternity, the living God is his *portion for ever* (v 26). Such communion with God is eternal life; death can neither disturb nor destroy it.

In conclusion, verses 27 and 28 summarize the contrasting destinies of the godly and the ungodly which the psalmist perceived in the sanctuary of God: *Those who are far from you will perish...but as for me, it is good to be near God.* No doubt nearness to God does not appear "good" to the materialist, since it may involve sorrow and suffering in the world. But those who prize true riches know that our real and eternal "good" is in God.

Psalm 84

The Courts of the Lord

The Temple in Jerusalem was for the Jew the most sacred spot on earth, for there in the Holy of Holies was the Shekinah glory, the visible manifestation of the presence of God. Of course the pious Israelite knew perfectly well, as Solomon had said, that God does not "dwell on earth" and that "the heaven, even the highest heaven cannot contain" him (1 Kings 8:27). Nevertheless, he had been pleased to "put his name" in Jerusalem and to cause the symbol of his presence to appear upon the mercy-seat behind

¹How lovely is your dwelling-place,
   O Lord Almighty!
²My soul yearns, even faints
   for the courts of the Lord;
my heart and my flesh cry out
   for the living God.
³Even the sparrow has found a
   home,
   and the swallow a nest for
   herself,
   where she may have her
   young—
a place near your altar,
   O Lord Almighty, my King and
   my God.
⁴Blessed are those who dwell in
   your house;
   they are ever praising you.
               Selah
⁵Blessed are those whose strength
   is in you,
   who have set their hearts on
   pilgrimage.
⁶As they pass through the Valley
   of Baca,
   they make it a place of springs;
   the autumn rains also cover it
   with pools.

⁷They go from strength to
   strength
   till each appears before God in
   Zion.
⁸Hear my prayer, O Lord God
   Almighty;
   listen to me, O God of Jacob.
               Selah
⁹Look upon our shield, O God;
   look with favor on your
   anointed one.
¹⁰Better is one day in your courts
   than a thousand elsewhere;
I would rather be a doorkeeper in
   the house of my God
   than dwell in the tents of the
   wicked.
¹¹For the Lord God is a sun and
   shield;
   the Lord bestows favor and
   honor;
no good thing does he withhold
   from those whose walk is
   blameless.
¹²O Lord Almighty,
   blessed is the man who trusts
   in you.

the veil of the Temple. As a result, every Israelite loved the Temple and looked forward eagerly to every chance to visit it, especially on the three annual festivals. He could sincerely sing: *How lovely is your dwelling-place, O LORD Almighty* (v 1). The same longing for the Temple is found in Psalms 42 and 43 and in some of the pilgrim psalms (120–134).

The blessedness of others (vs 1–7)

The psalmist begins by expressing how desirable God's dwelling-place is to him. His whole being longs for it, *soul, heart,* and *flesh.* He *yearns, even faints* for it, because to enter *the courts of the LORD* is equivalent to approaching *the living God* himself. But for some reason he is prevented from fulfilling his heart's desire. So he looks with envy upon those, both birds and humans, who can enjoy what at present is denied to him.

He thinks of the sparrows, the most numerous and common birds in the world, constructing their nests in every available nook and cranny of the Temple buildings. The *swallow* is probably the swift. Large numbers still visit Palestine on migration, and many nest even today in the precincts of the Mosque of Omar in Jerusalem. How fortunate these birds seem to the psalmist! They are permitted to dwell in the immediate proximity of the altars of God. Chattering sparrows and screaming swifts appear to unite with the people of God as they worship him. To them the writer now turns, the priests who *dwell* in God's house, always praising him (v 4), and the pilgrims who visit it from time to time. He pronounces them both *blessed* (vs 4, 5).

He concentrates on the pilgrims (vs 5–7), no doubt because he longs to be one himself, and gives a graphic description of their journey up to Jerusalem. They *have set their hearts on pilgrimage* (v 5), and their resolute purpose strengthens them on their arduous trek. He pictures them passing through an arid valley (*the Valley of Baca*). But even such forbidding parts of the journey do not deter the pilgrims. On the contrary, they find there *a place of springs* for *the autumn rains also cover it with pools.* In other words, "hope sustains them at every step" (Bishop Perowne). They go *from strength to strength*, fortified by the joyful expectation of appearing before God in Zion (v 7).

A personal prayer (vs 8-12)

As the psalmist describes the blessedness of sparrows and swifts, pilgrims and priests, who visit the Temple or dwell there, his own longing to join them breaks out into a prayer: *O Lord God Almighty, listen to me...* (v 8). There follows a prayer for God's *anointed one* (v 9), which must mean the king. We can only guess its relevance in this context. Perhaps it is that the nation's welfare was bound up in the king's.

The writer goes on to indicate the reason for his prayer to visit the Temple, and expresses it forcefully in terms of both time and space (v 10). One day in the courts of the Lord, he says, is to him better *than a thousand elsewhere*, while to be a mere *doorkeeper in the house of my God*, approaching only the threshold of the Temple, was preferable to dwelling at ease *in the tents of the wicked*. Only a day. Only a doorkeeper. And yet such a fleeting and distant contact with God would be satisfying, since he is a *sun*, bathing us with light, *and shield*, defending us from evil. More than that, he gives *favor and honor*; in fact *no good thing does he withhold from those whose walk is blameless* (v 11).

The psalm ends with another statement of who is *blessed*. It is not only the priests who dwell in the Temple precincts (v 4) and the pilgrims who visit them (v 5), but all people who put their trust in God (v 12), whether or not they have the opportunity to go up to Jerusalem.

Christian worshipers have no difficulty in applying this psalm to themselves, for the New Testament tells us plainly what the temple of God is which we may call *lovely* and make the object of our desire. First, it is the church, not only universal (Ephesians 2:21) but local (1 Corinthians 3:16; 2 Corinthians 6:16), that is, every company of believers. God does not dwell in temples made with hands (Acts 7:48) but among his people. We do not need to travel to Jerusalem to meet him. When only two or three of us have met in the name of Christ, he is there in our midst (Matthew 18:20). This is why we love to come together for public worship.

But the final fulfilment of the temple idea will be heaven, the new Jerusalem, of which it is written: "I did not see a temple in the city, because the Lord God Almighty and the Lamb are its temple," and "Now the dwelling of God is with men, and he will live with them. They will be his people, and God himself will be with them and be their God" (Revelation 21:22, 3). In this sense, too, Christian believers know in their own experience the psalmist's ardent longing for the temple of God. We thirst for God, and our Christian hope sustains us on our weary pilgrimage to heaven.

In his paraphrase of this psalm, Henry Francis Lyte skilfully combines the double New Testament application of the temple theme to Christian worship and to heaven:

> *Pleasant are your courts above,*
> *In the land of light and love;*
> *Pleasant are your courts below,*
> *In this land of sin and woe.*
> *Oh! my spirit longs and faints*
> *For the converse of your saints,*
> *For the brightness of your face,*
> *For your fulness, God of grace.*

Psalm 90

Life's Transient Dream

¹LORD, you have been our dwelling-
place
throughout all generations.
²Before the mountains were born
or you brought forth the earth
and the world,
from everlasting to everlasting
you are God.
³You turn men back to dust,
saying, "Return to dust, O sons
of men."
⁴For a thousand years in your
sight
are like a day that has just
gone by,
or like a watch in the night.
⁵You sweep men away in the
sleep of death;
they are like the new grass of
the morning—
⁶though in the morning it springs
up new,
by evening it is dry and
withered.
⁷We are consumed by your anger
and terrified by your
indignation.
⁸You have set our iniquities before
you,
our secret sins in the light of
your presence.
⁹All our days pass away under
your wrath;
we finish our years with a
moan.
¹⁰The length of our days is
seventy years—
or eighty, if we have the
strength;
yet their span is but trouble and
sorrow,
for they quickly pass, and we
fly away.
¹¹Who knows the power of your
anger?
For your wrath is as great as
the fear that is due you.
¹²Teach us to number our days
aright,
that we may gain a heart of
wisdom.
¹³Relent, O LORD! How long will it
be?
Have compassion on your
servants.
¹⁴Satisfy us in the morning with
your unfailing love,
that we may sing for joy and
be glad all our days.
¹⁵Make us glad for as many days
as you have afflicted us,
for as many years as we have
seen trouble.
¹⁶May your deeds be shown to
your servants,
your splendor to their children.
¹⁷May the favor of the LORD our
God rest upon us;
establish the work of our hands
for us—
yes, establish the work of our
hands.

This psalm sets out the brevity of human existence in the light of God's eternity. The author refers to some period of special affliction (v 15) as well as to humankind's universal frailty and sinfulness. Yet he betrays no sign of despair or complaint; his spirit is one of humble submission and trust.

God's eternity (vs 1–6)

The psalm opens with a magnificent statement of the eternity of God, because of which he has ever been the *dwelling-place* of his people. The word for *dwelling-place* is the same as that in Deuteronomy 33:27: "The eternal God is your *refuge*, and underneath are the everlasting arms." Amid all the ups and downs of life our only security is in him who, before the birth of the mountains and creation of the earth, indeed *from everlasting to everlasting*, is God.

Human beings are by contrast creatures of dust. In a clear allusion to Genesis 3:19, God is described as commanding them to return to dust (v 3). Such is the reality of death, "earth to earth, ashes to ashes, dust to dust". We are not only mortal, but extremely short-lived. To God a whole millennium is equivalent to a day (compare 2 Peter 3:8) or even to one of the watches of the night (v 4). But in comparison with the divine timelessness, our human life is *like the new grass*, which flourishes in the morning but is withered by the evening, scorched by sun and wind. This is a constant theme of Scripture, and other vivid metaphors are used to stress the brevity of our life on earth. It is like water spilt on the ground, like a shadow which passes when the sun comes out, and like smoke or mist dispersed by the wind.

God's wrath (vs 7–11)

In the next paragraph the thought moves on from God's eternity to his wrath. At first it may seem an abrupt transition, but the psalmist sees human mortality against the dark background of God's displeasure at sin. This is not only that the nation was passing through some calamity which he attributes to the judgment of God, but because he recognizes that death is the penalty for human sin (Genesis 2:17; 3:19; Romans 5:12). So he writes of our *iniquities* and even our *secret sins* being open before God (v 8), and says that *all our days pass away under your wrath* (v 9). Our average span of life may be 70 years, yet even these are *trouble and sorrow*. this is not said in bitterness, but in calm and sober realism. Every human being is destined to die, and our brief life span is spent under the judgment of God (v 11), unless and until we find mercy. This brings us naturally to the prayers with which the psalm concludes.

God's mercy (vs 12–17)

The first prayer inspired by a sense of human sin and mortality is in verse 12: *Teach us to number our days aright, that we may gain a heart of wisdom. Wisdom* consists of knowing and fearing God; life is so short that it is folly to ignore him. The rich farmer in the parable of Jesus, who planned and spoke as if life lasted for ever, God called a fool.

Secondly, *Satisfy us in the morning with your unfailing love,* for if we find our peace in the love of God early, we shall *be glad all our days* (vs 13, 14). Further, the joy God gives us will make up for the years of adversity (v 15).

The third prayer is concerned with our *work*. One of the tragedies of death is that it interrupts our labor and cuts short our achievement. This is true, however, only of human endeavor undertaken in human strength. When God shows *his work* to his servants, manifesting his power on their behalf and blessing them with his favor, the result is that he prospers *the work of our hands for us* (vs 16, 17). The only work which lasts is that which God establishes.

The brevity of life should still constrain us to get a heart of wisdom, namely to make God our refuge, to find rest in his love and fruitful labor under his blessing.

Psalm 91

The Defence of the Most High

This psalm has an unusual distinction: it is the only passage of Scripture which (at least in the sacred record) is quoted by the devil! (See Matthew 4:6 and Luke 4:10, 11.) This is more important than it sounds, because actually the devil misquoted it, or rather misapplied it. He urged the Son of God to throw himself down from the pinnacle of the Temple and trust God's promise (vs 11 and 12) that his angels would protect him, so that he

¹He who dwells in the shelter of
  the Most High
will rest in the shadow of the
  Almighty.
²I will say of the LORD, "He is my
  refuge and my fortress,
my God, in whom I trust."
³Surely he will save you from the
  fowler's snare
and from the deadly pestilence.
⁴He will cover you with feathers,
  and under his wings you will
  find refuge;
his faithfulness will be your
  shield and rampart.
⁵You will not fear the terror of
  night,
nor the arrow that flies by day,
⁶nor the pestilence that stalks in
  the darkness,
nor the plague that destroys at
  midday.
⁷A thousand may fall at your side,
ten thousand at your right
  hand,
but it will not come near you.
⁸You will only observe with your
  eyes
and see the punishment of the
wicked.
⁹If you make the Most High your
  dwelling—
even the LORD, who is my
  refuge—
¹⁰then no harm will befall you,
no disaster will come near your
  tent.
¹¹For he will command his angels
  concerning you
to guard you in all your ways;
¹²they will lift you up in their
  hands,
so that you will not strike your
  foot against a stone.
¹³You will tread upon the lion and
  the cobra;
you will trample the great lion
  and the serpent.
¹⁴"Because he loves me," says the
  LORD, "I will rescue him;
I will protect him, for he
  acknowledges my name.
¹⁵He will call upon me, and I will
  answer him;
I will be with him in trouble,
I will deliver him and honor him.
¹⁶With long life will I satisfy him
and show him my salvation."

would not hurt himself. The devil is not the only person who has attempted to misapply Psalm 91, as if it promised an unconditional security in any and every circumstance.

Our Lord knew, however, that to jump from the roof of the Temple on the basis of this psalm's promise of divine protection would be to tempt God. Only children of God who are living in the will of God can expect the protection of God. Even then, they have no guarantee of being shielded from all harm (see verse 15). What they know is that ultimately, whatever their circumstances may be, they are secure in God's love. Psalm 91 is, in fact, the Old Testament equivalent of Romans 8:31–39.

The best way to grasp the sequence of thought is to see that first the believer speaks to God (vs 1, 2); then the psalmist addresses the believer (vs 3–13); while finally God intervenes, speaking to the reader, and himself confirms the believer's assurance of security which is the theme of the psalm (vs 14–16).

The believer (vs 1, 2)

The believer's faith is grounded upon who God is. He is *the Most High* and *the Almighty* on the one hand (v 1), infinite in transcendence and power; but on the other he is *the LORD* (v 2), Yahweh, the covenant God of Israel, bound to his people by a solemn undertaking. To *rest in the shadow* of such a God is wisdom; he is the believer's *refuge* and *fortress*.

The psalmist (vs 3–13)

Having quoted this confession of faith, the psalmist now endorses it, encouraging believers in it and assuring them of their safety. Bold imagery is used to illustrate the divine defense which is promised. God will defend them as a mother bird hides her chicks under her wings; his *faithfulness* will be to them as a soldier's *shield* (v 4). What, then, are the perils from which believers will be delivered? They are variously described: *the fowler's snare...the deadly pestilence* (v 3), *the terror of night...the arrow...by day* (v 5), *the pestilence and the plague* (v 6).

It is perfectly possible to interpret this figurative language as referring to literal calamities. But some writers suggest that real demons are in view, derived perhaps from Babylonian sources.

Be that as it may, deliverance is plainly promised from all

evil. *Ten thousand* may succumb to it (v 7), and the *wicked* shall reap the *punishment* of their sins (v 8), but to those who make the Lord their refuge, it may be confidently asserted: *no harm will befall you* (vs 9, 10). God's angels will protect them (vs 11, 12; compare Psalm 34:7 and Hebrews 1:14), so that not even the *lion and the cobra...and the serpent* (v 13) shall be able to harm them. The snake is the subtlest and the lion the strongest of all creatures. It is not without significance that Satan is called "that ancient serpent" and depicted as prowling round "like a roaring lion" (Revelation 12:9; 20:1 and 1 Peter 5:8).

The Lord (vs 14–16)

Finally, the Lord himself is heard to speak, neither to the believer nor to the psalmist, but to the reader, approving the believer's faith and the psalmist's theme. Has the psalmist affirmed: *he will save you?* He is quite right. Twice God echoes the same words himself: *I will rescue...I will deliver* (vs 14, 15). Why? *Because he loves me.* God is the supreme object of the believer's love as well as faith, and it is to those who love God that the assurance is given that "in all things God works for their good" (Romans 8:28). Not that believers can afford to be idle and do nothing. They must trust God, and express their faith in prayer. Then God *will* answer them. The divine deliverance does not, however, always mean an escape from trouble; it sometimes means finding God with them *in trouble* (v 15). The final promise which God makes to his trusting servants is of *long life* and *salvation* (v 16). It is not impossible that, like the prophets, the psalmist wrote more than he knew, for the ultimate meaning of security is that eternal life and salvation which are found in Jesus Christ alone.

Psalm 95

An Invitation to Sing and to Hear

This psalm is a summons to the people of God, who know him as the *Rock* of their salvation (v 1), both to sing his praises and to hear his word. From at least as early as the fourth century A.D. it has been sung in many churches at the beginning of public worship.

An invitation to sing God's praise (vs 1–7)

In King Henry VIII's devotional primer, Psalm 95 is called "a song stirring to the praise of God." And what a stirring summons it is! In verses 1, 2, and 6 there are seven exhortations one after the other. Indeed, members of the congregation, no doubt gathered in the Temple courts, are represented as engaged in

> ¹Come, let us sing for joy to the Lord;
>   let us shout aloud to the Rock of our salvation.
> ²Let us come before him with thanksgiving
>   and extol him with music and song.
> ³For the Lord is the great God,
>   the great King above all gods.
> ⁴In his hand are the depths of the earth,
>   and the mountain peaks belong to him.
> ⁵The sea is his, for he made it,
>   and his hands formed the dry land.
> ⁶Come, let us bow down in worship,
>   let us kneel before the Lord our Maker,
> ⁷for he is our God
> and we are the people of his pasture,
>   the flock under his care.
>   Today if you hear his voice
> ⁸do not harden your hearts as you did at Meribah,
>   as you did that day at Massah in the desert,
> ⁹where your fathers tested and tried me,
>   though they had seen what I did.
> ¹⁰For forty years I was angry with that generation;
>   I said, "They are a people whose hearts go astray,
>   and they have not known my ways."
> ¹¹So I declared on oath in my anger,
>   "They shall never enter my rest."

mutual exhortation. They are inciting one another to worship and urging each other to sing the praises of God, since public worship is essentially congregational.

In this psalm we are given incentives as well as invitations to worship. We do not just hear the repetitive *let us*, but the added *for the LORD is . . .* giving us a reason for our praise. Not until we grasp who the Lord is, are we inwardly moved to worship him.

Who, then, is he? The answer of this canticle is that he is both *the great God* (v 3) and *our God* (v 7).

First, he is *the great God*. He is supreme in heaven (v 3), *the great King above all gods*. There is no need to assume that the psalmist credited them with an objective reality, for "all the gods of the nations are idols" (Psalm 96:5). God is also supreme on earth (vs 4, 5). Every dimension is included, in order to show that nothing is beyond the dominion of God. The depths of the earth, the heights of the mountains, and the broad expanses of sea and land are all his. They are *in his hand* (v 4), because *his hands formed them* (v 5). The hand that made the universe in the beginning still holds the universe today. God is the controller of the natural order because he was the creator of it.

Secondly, *he is our God* (v 7). Far above us in his greatness, he is yet close to us in his goodness. His majesty is tempered with mercy, and his glory with grace. Did he make the world? He made Israel, too. He is *the LORD our Maker* (v 6); see also Psalms 100:3; 149:2; Isaiah 51:13; 54:5). The Creator of all things is the Redeemer of his special people. He is our Shepherd as well, calling us *the people of his pasture* (v 7).

Psalm 95 makes it plain that our mood will change in worship according to which aspect of God is occupying our attention. In verses 1 and 2 the invitation is to make a joyful noise to the Lord and come into his presence with thanksgiving, *for the LORD is a great God*. Because of his greatness in creation, we may well shout aloud in jubilation. But in verse 6 the invitation is to *kneel before the LORD*. Why? *For he is our God* (v 7). Has this great God condescended to be our God, becoming our shepherd and calling us his sheep? Then this is no moment for exuberant hilarity, but rather for awe and wonder, as with bated breath we prostrate ourselves before him in reverence and humility.

With the end of verse 7 the mood changes again. The speaker changes too. So far the congregation have been exhorting one another; now God intervenes and speaks to his people himself.

An invitation to hear God's word (vs 8–11)

We are not only to open our lips to sing God's praise, but to open our ears to hear his word. It is noteworthy that those who are exhorted to hear God's voice have been described in the previous verse as *the flock under his care*, because of course a sheep should know the shepherd's voice. Compare John 10:2–4.

The early days of Israel are taken by God as a striking object lesson. A month or two after the Exodus, just before they reached Mount Sinai, the children of Israel camped at Rephidim. There was no water. So the people found fault with Moses: "Give us water to drink. Why did you bring us out of Egypt to kill us, our children and cattle with thirst?" Moses prayed to the Lord, and at his instruction struck the rock with the rod of God, and water gushed out. Moses then gave to this place two names, *Massah* meaning testing or temptation, and *Meribah* meaning quarreling or provocation. This story is recorded in Exodus 17:1–7.

Forty years later a similar crisis arose at Kadesh. Water was again miraculously provided for the people, when they complained to Moses. This place came to be known as *Meribah-Kadesh*, to distinguish it from the *Meribah* at Rephidim. This second story is recorded in Numbers 20:1–13.

God's people had tested their God. They had put him to the proof. Although they had seen his works, they had no faith in him. God had wonderfully rescued them from their bondage in Egypt. He later established his covenant with them, gave them his special revelation, and provided for them in the wilderness. Yet here they were rebeling against him, and doubting his love and goodness. No wonder we go on to read, *forty years I was angry with that generation.* God also described them as *a people whose hearts go astray* (v 10). Their wandering in the wilderness was an outward counterpart to their straying hearts. So great was Israel's sin, unbelief, and rebellion, that it aroused a feeling of revulsion in the heart and mind of God (v 11). God is revealed in Scripture as a God of love and wrath, of goodness and severity. He hates sin with an implacable hatred, while yet loving the sinner with an inextinguishable love.

The letter to the Hebrews makes these verses an urgent message for Christians today. "So the Holy Spirit says: 'Today, if you hear his voice, do not harden your hearts as you did in the rebellion, during the time of testing in the desert...'" (Hebrews 3:7, 8). It is today which is the day of salvation; we must beware lest we become "hardened by sin's deceitfulness" (Hebrews 3:13).

Psalm 98

Jehovah, the Savior-King

The occasion of this psalm is evidently some great national victory, which has been achieved by God's right hand and holy arm, and in the sight of the nations. Whether the divine victory was over Egypt or Babylon or some other foe, it certainly foreshadows that mightier salvation from sin, Satan, and death, which God has brought to us through Jesus Christ his Son. This is the most marvelous of the *marvelous things* (v 1) which God has done, and it prompts the people of God to keep singing a *new song*, new from ever fresh wonder at his grace. Christian songs of praise are fundamentally a rejoicing in the *marvelous things* which God has done.

The psalmist's call to praise is not only due to God's mighty acts of the past. He sees them also as evidence of the present reign of God, and as a pledge that he will set up his final kingdom of righteousness on earth. His threefold theme, therefore,

¹Sing to the LORD a new song,
  for he has done marvelous
    things;
his right hand and his holy arm
  have worked salvation for him.
²The LORD has made his salvation
    known
  and revealed his righteousness
    to the nations.
³He has remembered his love
  and his faithfulness to the
    house of Israel;
all the ends of the earth have seen
  the salvation of our God.
⁴Shout for joy to the LORD, all the
    earth,
  burst into jubilant song with
    music;

⁵make music to the LORD with the
    harp,
  with the harp and the sound of
    singing,
⁶with trumpets and the blast of
    the ram's horn—
  shout for joy before the LORD,
    the King.
⁷Let the sea resound, and all that
    is in it,
  the world, and all who live in it.
⁸Let the rivers clap their hands,
  let the mountains sing
    together for joy;
⁹let them sing before the LORD,
  for he comes to judge the earth.
He will judge the world in
    righteousness
  and the peoples with equity.

concerns God the Savior, the King, and the Judge. He invites God's people to sing to him as their Savior (vs 1–4), *all the earth* (v 4) to worship him as King (vs 4–6), and nature (sea, the world, rivers, and mountains) to do homage to him as the coming Judge (vs 7–9).

God the Savior (vs 1–3)

The victory of God which inspired the composition of this psalm was gained by himself alone. He had no human cooperation. He relied upon *his right hand and his holy arm* (v 1). Since "God is spirit" (John 4:24), he has no body, of course, and therefore neither hands nor arms. Nevertheless, these vivid anthropomorphic expressions symbolize both his strength and his direct intervention on behalf of his people. The redemption from Egypt and from Babylon are alike ascribed in Scripture to the strong arm or mighty hand of God (see for example Exodus 15:6,12; Psalm 44:1–3; and Isaiah 52:10; 59:16; 63:5).

Further, this victory of God was no secret affair, but rather a public spectacle. He *revealed* it in the sight of the nations (v 2). What they saw was his *salvation* and his *righteousness*.

God had also made known his *love and his faithfulness to the house of Israel* (v 4). Israel were God's chosen people, with whom he had entered into a solemn covenant. This covenant he would never break, nor forget. Indeed, the recent deliverance was a proof of his loyalty to it. So Israel could praise God not only for his power, which gained the victory, but for his faithfulness out of which it sprang. Although it was a victory gained for Israel by Israel's God, (*our God*), it had been seen by *all the ends of the earth* in fulfilment of the prophecy of Isaiah 52:10, which John the Baptist applied to the salvation of Jesus (Luke 3:6). The combination of *love* and *faithfulness* may also be seen throughout Psalm 89, in Psalms 92:2 and 100:5, and Micah 7:20.

God the King (vs 4–6)

If the people of Israel have been summoned to praise God, so now are the inhabitants of *all the earth* (v 4; compare Psalm 100:1). Even if they have not like Israel experienced his salvation, they can with Israel recognize his kingdom. He is *the LORD, the King* (v 6). His mighty deliverance of his people is a visible token of his sovereign rule over the affairs of human beings and nations. He is to be worshiped not merely with a *shout* (v 4), but with singing and musical instruments (vs 5, 6).

It seems likely that these outward expressions of rejoicing are chosen because they commonly accompanied the accession or coronation of a new king. When Zadok anointed Solomon king, they blew the trumpet, and the people shouted and rejoiced with music (1 Kings 1:39,40). Similarly, when the boy king Joash was crowned and anointed by Jehoiada the priest, there was a clapping of hands as well (2 Kings 11:12–14). So the reign of Jehovah is to be similarly celebrated with singing and shouting, with clapping of hands and blowing of trumpets (compare Psalm 47). There was in Hebrew worship what C.S. Lewis calls a certain "gusto".

God the Judge (vs 7–9)

In this worship of men and women, expressed jubilantly through musical instruments and the human voice, the whole range of animate and inanimate nature is now invited to join. The sea and its denizens, the world and its inhabitants, the floods and the hills are together to be joyful *before the LORD* (vs 6, 9). The roaring of the sea is its worship; in the splashing of the floods we can hear them clap their hands. The reason for their rejoicing lies yet in the future.

It seems to be recognized that nature is subject to some kind of bondage, as the apostle Paul was later to show in Romans 8:18–25, and it would be delivered only when God came to set up his kingdom. He is already King (v 6), but the earth does not yet acknowledge his rule. So he is coming to judge the earth, and its peoples (v 9). Only when God's rule is established on earth (as it has begun to be through Christ, although the Messianic kingdom is pictured in this psalm as a rule of Jehovah himself), will the peoples and nature itself be subdued and righteously governed. He who has already shown his righteousness in the saving of his people (v 2), will exhibit it again in his judging of the world. This judgment will include the punishment of the wicked, as is made plain in Isaiah 11:1–5. But even in this too we may rejoice, for we shall recognize that "true and just are his judgments", and concurring in them we shall cry, "Amen, Hallelujah!" (Revelation 19:1–5).

Psalm 100

The Lord is God and Good

This psalm was sung by the Israelites first in the Temple, and then in the daily synagogue services. The medieval church sang it in the service called Lauds. It is most popular today in its metrical version, "All people that on earth do dwell", which was probably composed by William Kethe, a sixteenth-century Scotsman and friend of the Reformer John Knox.

It has only five verses, but it is an eloquent summons to worship; and the worship to which it bids us is to have two marks.

Two characteristics of worship

This psalm is often called "the *Jubilate*", which means "O be joyful!" or "shout aloud!". Joy is to characterize our worship. Psalm 100 is one of a group of eight which celebrate the kingly sovereignty of Jehovah. "The LORD reigns, he is robed in majesty... Your throne was established long ago." "The LORD is the great God, the great King above all gods." "Say among the nations: 'The LORD reigns.'" "The LORD reigns, let the earth be glad." "Shout for joy before the LORD, the King." "The LORD reigns, let the nations tremble." (Psalms 93:1, 2; 95:3; 96:10; 97:1; 98:6; 99:1). Of these royal psalms the hundredth is the doxology.

For if God is king, what can our worship be but joyful? Away

---

¹Shout for joy to the LORD, all the earth,
² Serve the LORD with gladness; come before him with joyful songs.
³Know that the LORD is God. It is he who made us, and we are his; we are his people, the sheep of his pasture.

⁴Enter his gates with thanksgiving and his courts with praise; give thanks to him and praise his name.
⁵For the LORD is good and his love endures for ever; his faithfulness continues through all generations.

---

with funereal faces and doleful dirges! Joy, gladness, and singing
are to be the accompaniment of worship.

Our worship is to be universal as well as joyful. *Shout for joy
all the earth* (v 1). It is true that this psalm concerns Jehovah, the
God of Israel; but the psalmist realizes that he is not Israel's
monopoly. Had he not sworn to Abraham: "In your seed shall all
the families of the earth be blessed"? Is it not written in Isaiah
56:6, 7: "And foreigners who bind themselves to the Lord to serve
him, to love the name of the Lord … these will I bring to my holy
mountain and give them joy in my house of prayer'… for my
house will be called a house of prayer for all nations"? Then no
nation should stand aside from this call to worship. Jehovah is
not the tribal deity of Israel, but the sovereign Ruler over all the
earth. When we assemble for worship, therefore, we should
desire not only to make a joyful noise ourselves, but that all
nations should unite with us in our joyful task.

The rest of this psalm is devoted to an exposition of why the
nations should join us. Worship is not only to be joyful and universal, but reasonable.

The greatness of God

Know that the Lord is God (v 3). How we worship depends on what
we know. Knowledge and understanding play an important part
in our worship. Christians do not worship "an unknown God",
like the ancient Athenians, but a God who has revealed himself.

What then are we to know? The gods of the heathen are
idols; they can neither see, nor speak, nor act. Our God is a living and active God. Moreover, the chief evidence which the
psalmist gives of his activity is to be found in the history of
Israel. He redeemed his people from their bondage in Egypt,
entered into a covenant with them at Mount Sinai, led them
across the wilderness, and settled them in the Promised Land. In
a word he *made* them (compare Deuteronomy 32:6, 15 and Psalm
95:6). *It is he who made us, and we are his* (v 3). Of this sovereign,
intervening activity of God, two vivid illustrations are given.

First, God is the potter. *It is he who made us.* God is here
likened to a craftsman. It is not the individual, but the nation, to
which the phrase refers. Israel is sometimes called by God in the
Old Testament "the work of my hands" (see for example Isaiah
29:23; 60:21).

With what immense skill and patience did the divine potter

pursue his labor! His raw material was always unpromising, and often recalcitrant. Others would have long since abandoned all hope of success. But he persevered. Undeterred by any setback, and refusing to be discouraged by any disappointment, he went on fashioning Israel into a vessel of honor, fit for his own use.

Secondly, God is the shepherd. *We are his people, the sheep of his pasture.* The potter who made them was the shepherd who tended them. Through all the vicissitudes of their colorful career, he protected and guided them. He watched over them with all the conscientious tenderness of an eastern shepherd.

So it is with us also. God has redeemed us and brought us to himself. We can say that he is our potter and our shepherd. Nothing could indicate more clearly and emphatically than this what we owe to the sovereign grace of God. It is he who has made us and we are his people. We have neither created nor constituted ourselves the people of God. "By the grace of God we are what we are." What we are is therefore cause for praise, not for pride.

No wonder the psalmist bursts into another call to worship: *Enter his gates with thanksgiving and his courts with praise; give thanks to him and praise his name* (v 4). Our worship is to be joyful simply because it is grateful.

The goodness of God

The Lord is not only great, but *good* (v 5). There is ground to praise him not only for what he has done, but for what he is.

Wherein does his goodness consist? It consists in his love which *endures for ever* and his *faithfulness* (v 5). Our God is a covenant-keeping God. He is neither fickle nor faithless; his word is dependable, and his promises are trustworthy. From generation to generation he remains the same. From everlasting to everlasting he is God.

We are summoned to worship him not just because he has made us and taken us to himself to be his own, but because he will stay by us. The heavenly potter will never discard his work; he will persist in fashioning it into a vessel that is beautiful and useful. The heavenly shepherd will never abandon his sheep; he will make them lie down in green pastures and lead them beside still waters. His goodness and mercy will follow them all the days of their life. The vessel is safe in the potter's hand. The sheep are safe in the shepherd's arms.

Psalm 103

The Benefits of God's Grace

[1]Praise the LORD, O my soul;
  all my inmost being, praise his
    holy name.
[2]Praise the LORD, O my soul,
  and forget not all his benefits.
[3]He forgives all my sins
  and heals all my diseases;
[4]he redeems my life from the pit
  and crowns me with love and
    compassion.
[5]He satisfies my desires with good
    things,
  so that my youth is renewed
    like the eagle's.
[6]The LORD works righteousness
  and justice for all the
    oppressed.
[7]He made known his ways to
    Moses,
  his deeds to the people of
    Israel:
[8]The LORD is compassionate and
    gracious,
  slow to anger, abounding in
    love.
[9]He will not always accuse,
  nor will he harbor his anger for
    ever;
[10]he does not treat us as our sins
    deserve
  or repay us according to our
    iniquities.
[11]For as high as the heavens are
    above the earth,
  so great is his love for those
    who fear him;
[12]as far as the east is from the
    west,

so far has he removed our
    transgressions from us.
[13]As a father has compassion on
    his children,
  so the LORD has compassion on
    those who fear him;
[14]for he knows how we are formed,
  he remembers that we are dust.
[15]As for man, his days are like grass,
  he flourishes like a flower of
    the field;
[16]the wind blows over it and it is
    gone,
  and its place remembers it no
    more.
[17]But from everlasting to
    everlasting
  the LORD's love is with those
    who fear him,
  and his righteousness with
    their children's children—
[18]with those who keep his
    covenant
  and remember to obey his
    precepts.
[19]The LORD has established his
    throne in heaven,
  and his kingdom rules over all.
[20]Praise the LORD, you his angels,
  you mighty ones who do his
    bidding,
  who obey his word.
[21]Praise the LORD, all his heavenly
    hosts,
  you his servants who do his will.
[22]Praise the LORD, all his works
  everywhere in his dominion.
Praise the LORD, O my soul.

Psalm 103 is, undoubtedly, one of the best-loved psalms, just as Henry Francis Lyte's free paraphrase, "Praise my Soul, the King of heaven", is one of the most popular hymns in the English language. We have here the authentic utterance of a redeemed child of God, who piles up words to express his gratitude to the God of grace. His praise expands in three concentric circles. First, he addresses himself and seeks to arouse himself to the proper worship of God: *Praise the* LORD, *O my soul* (vs 1–5). Next, he recalls the mercy of God to all the people of his covenant (vs 6–18). Finally, he summons the whole of creation to join in the chorus of praise (vs 19–22).

God's benefits to me (vs 1–5)

The first five verses of the psalm are very personal, as the author confronts himself with his duty and exhorts his own sluggish soul to worship. He desires not only to praise God's *holy name* (v 1), acknowledging the holiness or unique "otherness" of his being, but to remember *all his benefits*. Indeed, he is determined that his worship of God shall be as total as are God's blessings to him: *all my inmost being* in response to *all his benefits*. These benefits have been given to both body and soul, for God both *forgives all my sins* and *heals all my diseases* (v 3). Further, he redeems my life *from the pit* (v 4), that is the grave or Sheol. Not content with saving the psalmist from sin, disease, and death, God lavishes positive blessings upon him as well. He *crowns* him (v 4), that is, he makes his child a king (compare Psalm 8:5).

God also satisfies him *with good things* (v 5), so that our *youth is renewed like the eagle's.* Maybe this alludes to an ancient fable that the eagle soars periodically so near to the sun that it drops scorched into the sea and emerges miraculously rejuvenated, or to the bird's annual molt and "eclipse" after the breeding season, until the plumage is renewed the following spring. Here, as in Isaiah 40:31, the eagle is used as a symbol of youth and strength.

These, then, are God's personal benefits to the psalmist. Delivered from sin, sickness, and death, he feels himself as privileged as a king and as vigorous as an eagle.

God's mercy to his people (vs 6–18)

The psalmist now changes from the singular to the plural, from the particular benefits which he has himself received to God's general grace to all the people of his covenant. Whenever they have been *oppressed* he has displayed on their behalf both *righteousness and justice* (v 6). The most signal revelation of this was to Moses and to the children of Israel under Moses' leadership (v 7). Such just dealing with his people was an expression of his grace.

Indeed, what the psalmist goes on to write is a kind of meditation on that glorious revelation of God's name to Moses: "The LORD, the LORD, the compassionate and gracious God, slow to anger, abounding in love and faithfulness" (Exodus 34:6). After quoting these words (v 8), our author proceeds to enforce them by two negative statements, three illustrations and a striking contrast.

The two negatives indicate that God sets limits to his own righteous wrath against sin. The first is a time limit, that he *will not always accuse*. The second is a restraint upon the expression of his anger that, instead of that just judgment, *he does not treat us as our sins deserve* (vs 9, 10). Then follow three positive illustrations of God's grace. His steadfast love is as high as heaven, his forgiveness removes our sins as far away as infinity, and his pity is as tender as a father's for his children, because he knows our human frailty (vs 11–14).

The mention of human weakness leads to the final underlining of the mercy of God, which, as in Psalm 90, takes the form of a contrast between human transience and the eternity of God's love. Humankind flourishes like grass, and perishes like grass too when the hot desert wind blows upon it; but toward those who reverence God, keep his covenant, and remember his commandments, his *love* and *righteousness* endure for ever and enrich their posterity (vs 15–18). This assurance of God's unfailing love to successive generations has brought comfort to many mourners as they have stood around the grave and watched a coffin lowered to its final resting place.

God's dominion over all creation (vs 19–22)

In the last paragraph the psalmist turns from the love of the Lord for his covenant people to his sovereignty over all his creation. He has *established his throne in heaven* and from there *rules over all* (v 19). Thus convinced of God's universal kingdom, the author summons the whole created order to praise him. First, he addresses the mighty *angels*, called also God's *hosts* and *servants*, whose characteristic activity is to *do his will* (vs 20, 21). Next he turns to the lower orders of God's creation and calls on *all his works everywhere* to worship him. Finally, he comes back to himself and concludes the psalm as he began it, with the personal exhortation: *Praise the Lord, O my soul* (v 22).

Psalm 104

The Works of God in Nature

¹Praise the LORD, O my soul.
O LORD my God, you are very
　　great;
　　you are clothed with splendor
　　and majesty.
²He wraps himself in light as with
　　a garment;
　　he stretches out the heavens
　　like a tent.
³　and lays the beams of his upper
　　chambers on their waters.
He makes the clouds his chariot
　　and rides on the wings of the
　　wind.
⁴He makes winds his messengers,
　　flames of fire his servants.
⁵He set the earth on its
　　foundations;
　　it can never be moved.
⁶You covered it with the deep as
　　with a garment;
　　the waters stood above the
　　mountains.
⁷But at your rebuke the waters
　　fled,
　　at the sound of your thunder
　　they took to flight;
⁸they flowed over the mountains,
　　they went down into the
　　valleys,
　　to the place you assigned for
　　them.
⁹You set a boundary they cannot
　　cross;
　　never again will they cover the
　　earth.
¹⁰He makes springs pour water
　　into the ravines;

it flows between the
　　mountains.
¹¹They give water to all the beasts
　　of the field;
　　the wild donkeys quench their
　　thirst.
¹²The birds of the air nest by the
　　waters;
　　they sing among the branches.
¹³He waters the mountains from
　　his upper chambers;
　　the earth is satisfied by the
　　fruit of his work.
¹⁴He makes grass grow for the
　　cattle;
　　and plants for man to
　　cultivate—
　　bringing forth food from the
　　earth:
¹⁵wine that gladdens the heart of
　　man,
　　oil to make his face shine,
　　and bread that sustains his
　　heart.
¹⁶The trees of the LORD are well
　　watered,
　　the cedars of Lebanon that he
　　planted.
¹⁷There the birds make their nests;
　　the stork has its home in the
　　pine trees.
¹⁸The high mountains belong to
　　the wild goats;
　　the crags are a refuge for the
　　coneys.
¹⁹The moon marks off the seasons,
　　and the sun knows when to go
　　down.

²⁰You bring darkness, it becomes
    night,
    and all the beasts of the forest
    prowl.
²¹The lions roar for their prey
    and seek their food from God.
²²The sun rises, and they steal
    away;
    they return and lie down in
    their dens.
²³Then man goes out to his work,
    to his labor until evening.
²⁴How many are your works,
    O LORD!
    In wisdom you made them all;
    the earth is full of your
    creatures.
²⁵There is the sea, vast and
    spacious,
    teeming with creatures
    beyond number—
    living things both large and
    small.
²⁶There the ships go to and fro,
    and the leviathan, which you
    formed to frolic there.
²⁷These all look to you
    to give them their food at the
    proper time.
²⁸When you give it to them,
    they gather it up;

when you open your hand,
    they are satisfied with good
    things.
²⁹When you hide your face,
    they are terrified;
when you take away their breath,
    they die and return to the dust.
³⁰When you send your Spirit,
    they are created,
    and you renew the face of the
    earth.
³¹May the glory of the LORD
    endure for ever;
    may the LORD rejoice in his
    works.
³²He looks at the earth, and it
    trembles;
    he touches the mountains, and
    they smoke.
³³I will sing to the LORD all my life;
    I will sing praise to my God as
    long as I live.
³⁴May my meditation be pleasing
    to him,
    as I rejoice in the LORD.
³⁵But may sinners vanish from the
    earth
    and the wicked be no more.
Praise the LORD, O my soul.
Praise the LORD.

Psalms 103 and 104 form a perfect pair and illustrate the balance of the Bible. Both begin and end with the words *Praise the LORD, O my soul.* Psalm 103 goes on to tell of the goodness of God in salvation, Psalm 104 of the greatness of God in creation (v 1). Psalm 103 depicts God as the father with his children, Psalm 104 as the Creator with his creatures. Psalm 103 catalogs his *benefits* (v 2), Psalm 104 his *works* (vs 13, 24, 31).

The author evidently has in mind the narrative of Genesis 1 and draws his inspiration from it. He follows approximately the same order, beginning with light and ending with human beings. He describes with great poetic beauty how God made the heavens and the earth (vs 1–9), and provides drink, food, and shelter for all birds and beasts (vs 10–23). After a further meditation on God's many varied works in both creating and preserving "all creatures great and small" (vs 24–30), he concludes with a prayer that God's glory may endure, a resolve to worship God throughout his life, and a desire that sinners who spoil God's world shall be no more (vs 31–35).

It is important to notice the form which the psalmist's "gusto for nature", as C.S. Lewis called it, took. He does not praise nature for its own sake; "there are no nature lyrics in the psalms. Nature is referred to only to the extent that it points to him who made everything" (C.S. Lewis). This emphasis is preserved in Sir Robert Grant's fine (if free) paraphrase, "O Worship the King" (1833).

God's creation of heaven and earth (vs 1–9)

Most of the verbs in this paragraph should probably be put in the past tense and understood to refer to the creation of the heavens (vs 1–4) and the earth (vs 5–9). We should beware of taking these verses literally. The author writes as a poet, not as a scientist. We are not intended to picture God riding on a chariot of clouds or building the earth like a house on actual, material foundations. All this is imagery.

What the passage does teach us is that God is the creator of the universe, and that he has revealed himself in it. In his essential being he is invisible, but he makes himself known in the visible order which he has made. The light is his garment, the heavens are his tent, the sky his chambers, and the clouds his chariot, while he makes the winds his messengers and fire and flame his servants (vs 2–4). "In comparing the light to a robe," comments the reformer John Calvin, "he signifies that, though God is invisible, yet his glory is manifest."

Similarly, the earth is described as having been established upon firm foundations and then covered with the deep. This is the primeval chaos, when "the earth was formless the empty" and "darkness was over the surface of the deep" (Genesis 1:2). Then the separation of earth from sea is dramatically portrayed (as in Genesis 1:9,10): the waters *flowed over the mountains, they went down into the valleys, to the place you assigned for them* (v 8).

God's provision for birds and beasts (vs 10–23)

In this part of the psalm the verbs are mostly in the present tense, and remind us that Christians are not deists. The nineteenth-century deists believed that God had wound up the universe and set it in motion like a gigantic clockwork toy. The Bible teaches, however, that God is a living God, ceaselessly active in the control and the care of what he has made. He makes provision for the *beasts of the field* and *the birds of the air* (vs 11, 12). "Ecology" would be a term too grandiosely scientific to apply to this paragraph; yet this is what the author is depicting. He is fascinated by God's marvelous adaptation of the earth's resources to the needs of living creatures, and vice versa.

Thus, the streams which flow through the valleys provide drink for the animals (vs 10, 11), while God's rain waters the mountains (v 13) and the trees (v 16). Similarly, humans and beasts are supplied with food from the earth, including wine, oil, and bread (vs 14, 15). Even carnivorous lions are said to seek their food from God (v 21).

Living creatures require more than food and drink, however; they need shelter also, to protect them from the fury of the elements and in their breeding season. So birds, which *sing among the branches* (v 12), also *make their nests in them* (v 17). Storks build *in the pine trees* (v 17), while *the high mountains* are a refuge *for the wild goats* and *the crags for the coneys* (v 18; this is also translated badger and rabbit; it is evidently a hyrax). Further safety is provided by the cover of darkness, when *all the beasts of the forest prowl*. Then, when *the sun rises... they steal away... and lie down in their dens*; whereas human beings, by contrast, work by day and sleep at night (vs 19–23).

God's creation and preservation of all creatures (vs 24–30)

The psalmist interrupts his descriptions with an outburst of praise (v 24). Both earth and sea teem with his creatures, *living things both large and small* (v 25). The sea is also the place of ships and the playground of Leviathan (v 26). The latter is evidently a great sea creature, which some scholars think "is the whale, some the porpoise; in Job 41 it is probably the crocodile". Whatever Leviathan is, God is represented in the Talmud as playing with it.

Further, if God has made all creatures in his wisdom, he also cares for them in his faithfulness. They *all look to you* (v 27). They depend upon him for their food and breath. Not that they are inactive in feeding themselves, for they have to *gather up* their food; but God *gives* it. This truth is further enforced by striking anthropomorphisms, which speak of God's *hand* and *face* (vs 28, 29). Just as we have seen a child at the zoo or in the farmyard, offering food to some animal on the palm of an outstretched hand, so God opens his hand, that his creatures may be *satisfied with good things*. But when he turns away from them and hides his face, *they are terrified*. When further, he takes away their breath, *they die and return to the dust*. When, on the other hand, he sends his Spirit (or "breath"), they are not only created in the first place, but continuously renewed.

Food and life are the basic needs of every creature, and here their presence is attributed to the open hand and quickening breath of God, their absence to his hidden face. To modern ears it all sounds very naive. Can we believe such things in this age of science and technology? We have already noted that the descriptive passages are figurative, whether in the use of poetic or of anthropomorphic imagery.

But the truth behind the figures stands. God the Creator is lord of his creation. He has not abdicated his throne. He rules what he has made. No Christian can have a mechanistic view of nature. The universe is not a machine which operates by inflexible laws, nor has God made laws to which he is himself now a slave. The very term "natural laws" is only a convenient expression for the observed consistency of God's working. He is living and active in his universe, and we depend upon him for our "life and breath and everything else" (Acts 17:25). It is right to thank him not only for our creation, but for our preservation as well.

In conclusion, the psalmist expresses the fervent wish that God's glory (seen in his works) may always endure, and that God may continue to rejoice in his works, as he did when they left his hand at the beginning (v 31; compare Genesis 1:31), lest he should look upon the earth with judgment instead of favor (v 32). The psalmist determines himself to spend his whole life praising God and hopes that this psalm, his meditation upon the works of God, may please him (vs 33, 34). Yet he recognizes that there are *sinners* and *wicked* people who do not give to God, their creator and preserver, the glory that is due to his name (v 35). The God in whose hand their breath is, they have not honored (Daniel 5:23). His earnest desire is that such sinners should no longer be permitted to deface God's good world.

Psalm 121

The Lord our Keeper

The fifteen psalms from 120 to 134 inclusive form a self-contained group. At one time they were probably a separate collection. Each is entitled *A Song of Ascents*, literally, "A Song of Goings-up". The most probable meaning of this term is that these psalms were sung by groups of pilgrims while they were "ascending" toward Jerusalem for one of the three major annual festivals. Each of these psalms, then, is a pilgrimage song. They are brief, and most of them show a great love for Zion and the Temple and an ardent desire for the peace and prosperity of Jerusalem. These little psalms all breathe a spirit of quiet, undaunted faith in Israel's God, *the Maker of heaven and earth* (Psalm 121:2; 124:7; 134:4).

As they approached the hills surrounding Jerusalem, Psalm 121 would be an obviously suitable song for pilgrims to sing.

In the opening two verses the psalmist speaks in the first person singular, *I*. To his question in verse 1 about the source of his help comes his answer: *My help comes from the LORD, the Maker of heaven and earth* (v 2). This sentence contains a remarkable combination of ideas, that Jehovah, the covenant God of Israel, is the creator of the universe. In verse 4 he is further described as the keeper of Israel, who neither slumbers nor sleeps. This,

---

¹I lift up my eyes to the hills—
where does my help come
from?
²My help comes from the LORD,
the Maker of heaven and earth.
³He will not let your foot slip—
he who watches over you will
not slumber;
⁴indeed, he who watches over
Israel
will neither slumber nor sleep.

⁵The LORD watches over you—
the LORD is your shade at your
right hand;
⁶the sun will not harm you by day,
nor the moon by night.
⁷The LORD will keep you from all
harm—
he will watch over your life;
⁸the LORD will watch over your
coming and going
both now and for evermore.

then, is the ground of the author's faith in God's ability to keep, namely the almighty power of the world's creator and the ceaseless vigilance of Israel's guardian.

Having talked to himself, the psalmist now addresses some fellow-pilgrim, and the rest of his song expresses variations on the theme of God's keeping power. Although our English translation conceals the fact by using the words *keep* and *watch over*, the same Hebrew word which they translate actually occurs six times (vs 3, 4, 5, twice in v 7, v 8). He who keeps the nation Israel is also the keeper of the individual Israelite (vs 4, 5). He will keep him *from all harm*, watch over his *life* and his *coming and going...for evermore* (vs 7, 8).

Psalm 122

The Peace of Jerusalem

This psalm is, more obviously than all the other "Songs of Ascents", a song for pilgrims going up to Jerusalem for one of the feasts.

The first verse expresses the thrill the psalmist felt when he was invited to join the pilgrimage. By verse 2 he and the other pilgrims have arrived at their destination. Different thoughts begin to crowd into his mind as he looks round about him. He notices how *closely compacted* the city is (v 3). He also recalls God's purpose that the tribes should visit it for the yearly festivals *according to the statute given to Israel*, referring no doubt to the law recorded in Exodus 23:17. He remembers that Jerusalem is the centre of the nation's religious and political life, where the people may either praise the Lord or approach the *thrones for judgment*, if they have some dispute or law suit pending (vs 4, 5).

After his meditation, the psalmist breaks out into a plea that people will pray for the peace of Jerusalem, and he gives them a prayer to use (vs 6, 7). Having asked others to pray, he now prays himself. For the sake of his fellow-pilgrims and *for the sake of the house of the LORD our God* (which, above all, makes Jerusalem so precious), he will seek her *prosperity* (vs 8, 9).

¹I rejoiced with those who said to me,
  "Let us go to the house of the LORD."
²Our feet are standing
  in your gates, O Jerusalem.
³Jerusalem is built like a city
  that is closely compacted together
⁴That is where the tribes go up,
  the tribes of the LORD,
to praise the name of the LORD
  according to the statute given to Israel.
⁵There the thrones for judgment stand,
the thrones of the house of David.
⁶Pray for the peace of Jerusalem:
  "May those who love you be secure.
⁷May there be peace within your walls
  and security within your citadels."
⁸For the sake of my brothers and friends,
  I will say, "Peace be within you."
⁹For the sake of the house of the LORD our God,
  I will seek your prosperity.

Psalm 123

The Uplifted Eyes of Faith

The background of this psalm is the scornful opposition of the *proud* and the *arrogant* (v 4). We can only guess to whom the author is referring. It may have been any of Israel's enemies. But it certainly fits Sanballat the Horonite, Tobiah the Ammonite, and Geshem the Arab, who, when they heard of the Jews' resolve to rebuild the city wall, derided and despised them (see Nehemiah 2:19; 4:1–5).

The opening verses give a beautiful picture of quiet, patient confidence in the God who is enthroned in heaven (v 1). As the servant's eyes look to the hand of his master, and the maid's to her mistress's, *so our eyes look to the LORD our God* (v 2). This eye-to-hand gaze, as the analogy demands, expresses a waiting not for instructions but for provisions. It symbolizes dependence, not obedience.

Having declared that he is patiently waiting for God's mercy, the psalmist now prays for it. His prayer is not an individual one; he identifies himself with the nation: *we have endured much ridicule from the proud.*

---

¹I lift up my eyes to you,
  to you whose throne is in
    heaven.
²As the eyes of slaves look to the
    hand of their master,
  as the eyes of a maid looks to
    the hand of her mistress,
so our eyes look to the LORD our
    God,
  till he shows us his mercy.

³Have mercy on us, O LORD, have
    mercy on us,
  for we have endured much
    contempt.
⁴We have endured much ridicule
    from the proud,
  much contempt from the
    arrogant.

Psalm 125

The Mountains around Mount Zion

Most of Palestine is mountainous terrain, and mountains played an important part in the history of Israel. The pilgrims approaching Jerusalem naturally sang about them (see also Psalm 121:1).

Two mountain metaphors are combined. First, believers are like Mount Zion itself, standing firm. Secondly, they are like Jerusalem encircled by mountains, for they are themselves surrounded by the protection of Jehovah. Thus, God's people are like a mountain surrounded by mountains, both immovable and impregnable (vs 1, 2).

The metaphors are now applied. God will not allow *the scepter of the wicked* (v 3), which may refer to the machinations of the Persian-dominated Samaritans, to rule in the land which he has *allotted to the righteous*, lest the righteous *use their hands to do evil*. On the contrary, the psalmist prays with confidence that God will *do good ... to those who are good*, but drive away the evildoers (vs 4, 5).

---

¹Those who trust in the LORD are like Mount Zion,
which cannot be shaken but endures for ever.
²As the mountains surround Jerusalem.
so the LORD surrounds his people
both now and for evermore.
³The scepter of the wicked will not remain
over the land allotted to the righteous,

for then the righteous might use their hands to do evil.
⁴Do good, O LORD, to those who are good,
to those who are upright in heart.
⁵But those who turn to crooked ways
the LORD will banish with the evildoers.
Peace be upon Israel.

Psalm 127

The Vanity of Unblessed Labor

It is useless to launch a new enterprise or attempt to guard an old one, unless the Lord blesses these labors (v 1). The house builder's labor is vain unless the Lord does the building, and the city watchman's vigilance is vain unless the Lord does the watching. We may toil and overwork, getting up early and going to bed late, but all the time, if we only knew it, God *grants sleep to those he loves* (v 2) or "gives to his beloved in sleep" (Revised Standard Version). This, of course, is not a condemnation of industry, any more than our Lord's teaching in Matthew 6:25–34 is a prohibition of prudent forethought. What is condemned is worry on the one hand, and feverish self-confident activity on the other. Both are symptoms of unbelief.

Children must be recognized as *a heritage from the LORD* (v 3), one of God's most precious gifts. *Sons born in one's youth are like arrows* (v 4), for by the time their warrior father is aged they themselves will be old enough to defend and protect him. Moreover, if his *quiver is full of them*, he will be able to hold his own in any disputes *in the gate*, that is, in the space near the city gate where business is transacted and lawsuits are heard.

---

¹Unless the LORD builds the house,
  its builders labor in vain.
Unless the LORD watches over the city,
  the watchmen stand guard in vain.
²In vain you rise early
  and stay up late,
toiling for food to eat—
  for he grants sleep to those he loves.

³Sons are a heritage from the LORD,
  children a reward from him.
⁴Like arrows in the hands of a warrior
  are sons born in one's youth.
⁵Blessed is the man
  whose quiver is full of them.
They will not be put to shame
  when they contend with their enemies in the gate.

Psalm 130

Out of the Depths

The author's experience of forgiveness leads him to urge Israel to trust God for redemption.

The psalmist depicts himself as floundering in deep waters, and *out of the depths* he appeals to God to rescue him (vs 1, 2). These deep waters are a picture of his sin, guilt, and sense of God's judgment—his own, and perhaps the nation's too, with which he identifies himself (compare Nehemiah 1:4-7). The author knows that if God *kept a record of sins*, taking them into account and reckoning them up against him, neither he nor anyone else *could stand* (v 3). *But with you*, he immediately adds, *there is forgiveness* (v 4).

It was this offer of forgiveness by grace without works, which led Luther to call this penitential song one of the "Pauline Psalms". Verse 4 was also one of the Scripture verses which brought comfort to John Bunyan, author of *Pilgrim's Progress*, when he was convicted of sin. It contains a beautiful balance, because its first part brings assurance to the despairing, while its second part sounds a warning to the presumptuous. Far from encouraging sinners in their sins, God's forgiveness promotes that fear of the Lord, or reverent awe in his presence, which leads men and women to depart from iniquity (compare Proverbs 16:6).

---

¹Out of the depths I cry to you,
    O LORD;
² O Lord, hear my voice.
Let your ears be attentive
    to my cry for mercy.
³If you, O LORD, kept a record of
    sins,
    O LORD, who could stand?
⁴But with you there is forgiveness;
    therefore you are feared.
⁵I wait for the LORD, my soul waits,
    and in his word I put my hope.

⁶My soul waits for the LORD
    more than watchmen wait for
    the morning,
    more than watchmen wait for
    the morning.
⁷O Israel, put your hope in the
    LORD,
    for with the LORD is unfailing
    love
    and with him is full redemption.
⁸He himself will redeem Israel
    from all their sins.

Confident of the forgiving mercy of God to sinners, the author now does two things. First, he affirms his own determination to trust God for it. The ground of his faith is God's promise (v 5). Thus assured, his soul *waits for the* LORD (v 6). His guilty conscience has brought him into the darkness, but he longs and waits expectantly for the dawn of God's pardoning grace. Secondly, he urges Israel to do the same. His conviction regarding his own forgiveness (v 4) leads him to affirm that *with the* LORD *is unfailing love* for Israel's sin as well (v 7).

Psalm 131

A Child-like Humility

These words, which paint the picture of a little child's contented dependence on its mother, seem to anticipate our Lord's insistence on the necessity of a child-like humility.

The psalmist contrasts what he is not with what he is. He is not haughty, he says, in either heart or looks. He does not occupy himself with *great matters* (v 1). That is, he has renounced proud ambitions for prestige and power, whether for himself personally or for Israel after the Restoration, still humiliated under a foreign yoke. Instead, he is willing to be like a *weaned child*, no longer crying to be suckled, yet nestling contentedly at its mother's breast (v 2). The condition thus pictorially described seems to be a person (or nation) who, weaned from arrogant ambitions, finds perfect satisfaction in God. It is a beautiful picture not only of humble faith but of what might be called the "motherhood" of God.

As in Psalm 130, the psalmist leaves is description of the lesson he has learned and urges Israel to learn it too. *O Israel, put your hope in the LORD both now and evermore* (v 3).

---

¹My heart is not proud, O LORD,
  my eyes are not haughty;
I do not concern myself with
  great matters
  or things too wonderful for me.
²But I have stilled and quieted my
  soul;

like a weaned child with its
  mother,
like a weaned child is my soul
  within me.
³O Israel, put your hope in the
  LORD
  both now and for evermore.

Psalm 133

Brothers Dwelling in Unity

The unity of the people of God has always been both his will and the object of their desire. If this psalm is post-Exilic, it may express the joy and solidarity of pilgrims gathered for worship in Jerusalem, with the breach of the divided monarchy healed.

The covenant people of God are already *brothers*; but it is both *good and pleasant* if, in addition to their fraternal relationship, they *live together in unity* (v 1). The pleasantness of unity is now vividly illustrated. It is like the consecrating oil *running down on Aaron's beard* (from his head on which it had been poured) and flowing down on to the *collar of his robes*, and like *the dew of Hermon*, an expression for heavy dew (vs 2, 3).

We are not told why the unity of the people of God is like Aaron's consecrating oil and Hermon's heavy dew. Some writers have emphasized that both are said to descend, and that their significance is the all-embracing influence of true brotherly concord, sanctifying the whole body. At the same time, since aromatic oil will have been used and the dew was essential to the fertility of arid Palestine, these similes are surely meant also to teach that unity is as fragrant as oil and as refreshing as dew in Jerusalem. It is there that Jehovah *bestows blessing, even life for evermore* (v 3).

---

¹How good and pleasant it is
   when brothers live together in
     unity!
²It is like precious oil poured on
    the head,
   running down on the beard,
running down on Aaron's beard,
   down upon the collar of his
     robes.
³It is as if the dew of Hermon
   were falling on Mount Zion.
For there the LORD bestows his
    blessing,
   even life for evermore.

Psalm 139

The All-seeing Eye of God

¹O Lᴏʀᴅ, you have searched me
and you know me.
²You know when I sit and when I
rise;
you perceive my thoughts from
afar.
³You discern my going out and my
lying down;
you are familiar with all my
ways.
⁴Before a word is on my tongue
you know it completely, O Lᴏʀᴅ.
⁵You hem me in, behind and
before;
you have laid your hand upon
me.
⁶Such knowledge is too wonderful
for me,
too lofty for me to attain.
⁷Where can I go from your Spirit?
Where can I flee from your
presence?
⁸If I go up to the heavens, you are
there;
if I make my bed in the depths,
you are there.
⁹If I rise on the wings of the dawn,
if I settle on the far side of the
sea,
¹⁰even there your hand will guide
me,
your right hand will hold me
fast.
¹¹If I say, "Surely the darkness will
hide me
and the light become night
around me,"
¹²even the darkness will not be
dark to you;
the night will shine like the day,
for the darkness is as light to
you.
¹³For you created my inmost
being;
you knit me together in my
mother's womb.
¹⁴I praise you because I am
fearfully and wonderfully
made;
your works are wonderful,
I know that full well.
¹⁵My frame was not hidden from
you
when I was made in the secret
place.
When I was woven together in the
depths of the earth,
¹⁶ your eyes saw my unformed
body.
All the days ordained for me
were written in your book
before one of them came to be.
¹⁷How precious to me are your
thoughts, O God!
How vast is the sum of them!
¹⁸Were I to count them,
they would outnumber the
grains of sand.
When I awake
I am still with you.
¹⁹If only you would slay the
wicked, O God!
Away from me, you
bloodthirsty men!
²⁰They speak of you with evil
intent;

your adversaries misuse your name. ²¹Do I not hate those who hate you, O LORD, and abhor those who rise up against you? ²²I have nothing but hatred for them; I count them my enemies.	²³Search me, O God, and know my heart; test me and know my anxious thoughts. ²⁴See if there is any offensive way in me, and lead me in the way everlasting.

This has been called "the crown of all psalms." It is certainly a sublime exposition of one man's personal awareness of God's universal knowledge and presence. It is best known for verses 6 to 11, which unfold the impossibility of escape from God.

God's omniscience (vs 1–6)

The verbs paint a picture of God's perfect knowledge of humankind. He "searches", "knows", "perceives", "discerns", and is "familiar with" everything about us (vs 1–3). The divine knowledge extends to our thoughts, deeds, and words. First, God knows our thoughts *from afar* (v 2). "Neither space nor time exist for God" (Bishop Perowne); all human thoughts are open before him. Next, God perceives *all my ways*, including the activities of the day and the rest of the night (vs 2, 3). Thirdly, God knows the words of our tongue, even before they are spoken (v 4).

In verse 5, the psalmist begins to anticipate the theme of the next paragraph and attributes God's knowledge of him to his constant presence both *behind and before*. He pictures himself as a beleaguered city. But this encompassing presence of God fills him with wonder, not fear, and he breaks out in praise of God's amazing, unattainable knowledge (v 6).

God's omnipresence (vs 7–12)

This section begins with a question: *Where can I go from your Spirit?* (v 7). It is important to observe, however, that this question expresses not the desire to escape, but the joyful astonishment that escape is impossible and that God's hand is everywhere to guide and hold him (v 10). In order to emphasize the impossibility of escape from God, he mentions three conceivable escape routes or hiding places and declares that even there God is present. Thus, if he should ascend to heaven or

descend to Sheol, the abode of the dead, God is there (v 8). If he
should *rise on the wings of the dawn*, a beautiful figure of speech
for traveling at the speed of light, and reach *the far side of the sea*,
even there too he would find God. No distance, from farthest
east to farthest west, can separate him from God (vs 9, 10). Next,
if he should try to hide from God in the darkness, he would dis-
cover that God's eyes pierce through the gloom, since to God
darkness is as light (vs 11, 12).

God's omnipotence (vs 13–18)

God's omniscience, which in the previous section has been attributed to his omnipresence, is now attributed to his omnipotence.
God can search man out not only because he sees him, but because
he made him. The Creator knows his creatures through and
through. The psalmist ascribes the wonderful development of the
embryo in the womb to the creative power of God. Both his *inmost
being* and his *frame* (vs 13, 15) are God's. These together compre-
hend human beings, our body and our mind, emotions and will.
The phrase *fearfully and wonderfully made* (v 14), was originally
suggested by the translator Miles Coverdale, but may be incorrect.
Other modern translations render the phrase "for thou art fearful and wonderful". This wonderful creator-God, while fashioning
the writer, naturally saw his *unformed body* (v 16). More than that,
even before he was born, all the days of his life were planned and
recorded in God's book (vs 15, 16). Such divine knowledge and
foreknowledge cause the psalmist to burst into praise. For the
thoughts of God, which he calls *preciousand vast*, outnumber *the
grains of sand* (vs 17, 18).

He ends the paragraph with a statement whose meaning is
doubtful: *When I awake, I am still with you* (v 18). Some writers
suppose that he is referring again, as in the first two verses, to
God's continuous presence with him whether he wakes or sleeps.
Others think that he is referring to awaking from the sleep of
death.

God's judgment (vs 19–24)

If only you would slay the wicked, O God! (v 19). Many Christian
readers feel that this sudden prayer sounds a jarring note after
what has gone before. Yet it is perfectly consistent with it. When
a person's world is full of God, they long for the elimination of

evil. These evildoers are described both as *bloodthirsty* (v 19) and as those who misuse God's name (v 20), either taking his name in vain or exalting themselves against his authority. That is, they set themselves against both God and their fellows. In utter revolt against God's two great commandments to love him and their neighbor, they do not even stop short of blood (violence, murder) or of blasphemy.

This, then, is the first point to notice. The psalmist is not expressing feelings of personal animosity or revenge. He has come to count God's enemies (v 20) as his own enemies (v 22). He is righteously indignant, where we would be unrighteously tolerant. He burns with a divine hatred of sin.

But, it may be said, this man failed to distinguish between evil and the evildoer. Should he (and we with him) not learn to love the sinner and hate the sin? Of course there is some truth in this. Yet it can be overpressed, for "evil" is not something abstract; it exists in the hearts and ways of evildoers. So when the judgment of God falls, it will fall upon evildoers, not upon evil in the abstract.

But, an objector may further ask, while hope remains we should surely desire not judgment of sinners, but their salvation? Yes indeed, but what if sinners refuse to repent? We cannot desire their salvation in defiance of their own willingness to receive it. This is the heart of the matter. The Bible teaches that the sinner is at one and the same time the object of God's love and wrath (compare John 3:16, 36), and we should seek by grace at least to approximate our attitude to God's. We should earnestly desire the salvation of sinners if they will repent, and equally earnestly their (and indeed our own) destruction if they (or we) will not. It is because we find it difficult if not impossible to feel such sentiments, in divine purity without any admixture of personal venom, that we cannot easily echo the psalmist's words. But let us acknowledge the reason: it is because we know little of a truly righteous indignation.

Psalm 145

In Praise of God's Kingdom

The "kingdom" of God is the rule of God, both generally over the universe and particularly over his people, and it is this that is celebrated in Psalm 145. It is an acrostic psalm, each verse beginning with a different letter of the Hebrew alphabet in sequence, but its one theme is the glory and graciousness of Jehovah's rule. The praise which he deserves from his citizens is eternal and rational.

Eternal praise (vs 1-7)

The psalm opens with the author's resolve to exalt and praise God not only *every day* (v 2) but *for ever and ever* (vs 1, 2). Because the Lord is great, he is *most worthy of praise* (v 3); since *no-one can fathom* his greatness, his praise must be unceasing. But no individual can worship God for ever on earth. So the author seems to be speaking as the representative of Israel and to be referring to future generations, each of which will declare God's work to the next and so perpetuate his praise (v 4). They will be occupied with *your wonderful works, your awesome works, your great deeds* (vs 5-7).

Universal praise (vs 8-13)

The praise which is due to God is also universal, offered to him by all his creatures. This is only logical, because *he has compassion on all he has made* (v 9). The glory that is given by human beings to God is a response to the grace that is given to them by God. And God gives grace because he is gracious. Ultimately, both the eternity and the universality of worship arise from the gracious character of God. Verse 8 echoes Jehovah's self-revelation to Moses recorded in Exodus 34:6 and already quoted in Psalm 103:8. His nature of grace and mercy expresses itself in universal goodness to humankind (v 9). Hence the universality

¹I will exalt you, my God the King;
  I will praise your name for ever
    and ever.
²Every day I will praise you
  and extol your name for ever
    and ever.
³Great is the LORD and most
    worthy of praise;
  his greatness no-one can
    fathom.
⁴One generation will commend
    your works to another;
  they will tell of your mighty
    acts.
⁵They will speak of the glorious
    splendor of your majesty,
  and I will meditate on your
    wonderful works.
⁶they will tell of the power of
    your awesome works,
  and I will proclaim your great
    deeds.
⁷They will celebrate your
    abundant goodness
  and joyfully sing of your
    righteousness.
⁸The LORD is gracious and
    compassionate,
  slow to anger and rich in love.
⁹The LORD is good to all;
  he has compassion on all he has
    made.
¹⁰All you have made will praise
    you, O LORD;
  your saints will extol you.
¹¹They will tell of the glory of
    your kingdom
  and speak of your might,
¹²so that all men may know of
    your mighty acts

and the glorious splendor of
    your kingdom.
¹³Your kingdom is an everlasting
    kingdom,
  and your dominion endures
    through all generations.
The LORD is faithful to all his
    promises
  and loving towards all he has
    made.
¹⁴The LORD upholds all those who
    fall
  and lifts up all who are bowed
    down.
¹⁵The eyes of all look to you,
  and give them their food at the
    proper time.
¹⁶You open your hand
  and satisfy the desires of every
    living thing.
¹⁷The LORD is righteous in all his
    ways
  and loving towards all he has
    made.
¹⁸The LORD is near to all who call on
    him,
  to all who call on him in truth.
¹⁹He fulfills the desires of those
    who fear him;
  he hears their cry and saves
    them.
²⁰The LORD watches over all who
    love him,
  but all the wicked he will
    destroy.
²¹My mouth will speak in praise of
    the LORD.
  Let every creature praise his
    holy name for ever and ever.

of his praise. Human beings sing the glory, the power, and the eternity of his kingdom (vs 11–13). The words anticipate the doxology at the end of the Lord's Prayer: "Yours is the kingdom and the power and the glory for ever. Amen" (Matthew 6:13).

Rational praise (vs 14–21)

The praise which is to ascend to God for all time and from all people is intelligent worship, or what the Lord Jesus called "worship…in truth" (John 4:24). The only worship which is acceptable to God is offered in rational response to his revelation of himself. That is, it is a worship of his *name* (vs 1, 2, 21), his eternal being as made known in his words and works.

The psalmist now gives some concrete examples of God's gracious works. They show that his rule, though powerful, is not arbitrary. On the contrary, his kingdom is a beneficent kingdom, and his throne a throne of grace. See how he condescends to succor his people in all their need. He upholds the falling and raises the fallen (v 14). He feeds the hungry and satisfies *the desires of every living thing* (vs 15, 16). He comes close to those who call upon him; he hears and answers their prayers (vs 18, 19). He protects those who love him, but *will destroy* the wicked (v 20).

It is noteworthy that in verses 19 and 20 God's people are said both to *fear* and to *love* him. One writer comments: "Fear and love are the inseparable elements of true religion. Fear preserves love from degenerating into presumptuous familiarity: love prevents fear from becoming a servile and cringing dread."

The last verse (v 21) seems to summarize the three characteristics of the worship of Jehovah, which have been elaborated in the psalm. It is eternal (*for ever and ever*), universal (*every creature*), and rational (*praise his holy name*).

Psalm 150

The Final Doxology

The Psalter's doxology forms a fitting conclusion. As a summons to worship it is unsurpassed in grandeur. In common with the Hallel (Psalms 113–118) and the four preceding psalms (146–149), it begins and ends with the word Hallelujah or *Praise the LORD*. Further, every verse is an invitation to praise, telling us where and why, how and by whom, the praise of God should be expressed.

Where and why (vs 1, 2)

Praise God in his sanctuary. The catalogue of musical instruments which follows clearly relates to Temple worship. But God is to be praised *in his mighty heavens* too (v 1). So probably this verse is an invitation to both humans and angels to worship God— humans in earth's sanctuary, and angels in heaven. It reminds us that the praise of God is one, the church below joining "angels and archangels and all the company of heaven" in his worship.

The reasons why God is to be praised are found in his works and his nature, his doing and his being (v 2). His *acts of power* are not specified, but will include his works of creation, preservation, providence, and redemption. They are the expression of his

---

¹Praise the LORD.
Praise God in his sanctuary;
   praise him in his mighty
   heavens.
²Praise him for his acts of power;
   praise him for his surpassing
   greatness.
³Praise him with the sounding of
   the trumpet,
   praise him with the harp and
   lyre,
⁴praise him with tambourine and
   dancing,
   praise him with the strings and
   flute,
⁵praise him with the clash of
   cymbals,
   praise him with resounding
   cymbals.
⁶Let everything that has breath
   praise the LORD.
Praise the LORD.

---

surpassing greatness. This is the perennial theme of worship—the greatness of God displayed in his works.

How and by whom (vs 3-6)

Every conceivable instrument is to be employed in the worship of Jehovah: wind, strings, and percussion (compare Psalm 81:1-3). The first is *the trumpet*, the ancient curved ram's horn. This is "the only musical instrument still in use in the synagogue", writes one commentator, "and the expert can make a prodigious noise with it". The other two instruments mentioned in verse 3 are stringed, *the harp and lyre*. Next come the *tambourine and dancing* (v 4), and then *the strings and flute*, the latter being perhaps the simple shepherd's pipe. Verse 5 mentions two cymbals; the first possibly as small as castanets, the second larger and thus *resounding*.

So the orchestra is assembled. Worshipers are to blow the horn and pluck the harp, beat the drums, sweep the strings, play the flute, and clang the cymbals. "Noise, you may well say. Mere music is not enough... Let us have clashing cymbals, not only well tuned, but *loud*, and dances too," writes C.S. Lewis. What is here described is the uninhibited exuberance of lives devoted to God.

Nevertheless, the mere noise of instruments and movements of dancing are not acceptable to God, however beautiful, unless they express the devotion of our hearts and minds. The psalm's concluding verse (6), which calls on *everything that has breath* to praise God, may be intended to include the animal creation. Yet the emphasis is upon us human beings, the crown of God's creation, into whom he breathed the breath of life (Genesis 2:7). Our worship is not to be confined to church services. On the contrary, while we breathe, we praise.

Luke 1:68–79

The *Benedictus*

God's Mighty Salvation

Of the nine canticles appointed for regular use in the Episcopalian Church at Morning or Evening Prayer three come from the birth and infancy narratives of St Luke (*Benedictus, Magnificat, Nunc Dimittis*). These Gospel canticles have been loved and used by Christian people from the earliest days. In the medieval service of Lauds the *Benedictus* followed the lesson, although this usually consisted of no more than a verse or two. However, when Archbishop Thomas Cranmer lengthened the New Testament lesson to a full chapter, the *Benedictus* appropriately retained its place, enabling the congregation to praise God for the glorious fulfillment in Christ of all the Old Testament anticipation.

---

[68]Praise be to the Lord, the God of Israel,
because he has come and has redeemed his people.
[69]He has raised up a horn of salvation for us
in the house of his servant David
[70](as he said through his holy prophets of long ago),
[71]salvation from our enemies
and from the hand of all who hate us—
[72]to show mercy to our fathers
and to remember his holy covenant,
[73] the oath he swore to our father Abraham:
[74]to rescue us from the hand of our enemies,
and to enable us to serve him without fear

[75] in holiness and righteousness before him all our days.
[76]And you, my child, will be called a prophet of the Most High;
for you will go on before the Lord to prepare the way for him,
[77]to give his people the knowledge of salvation
through the forgiveness of their sins,
[78]because of the tender mercy of our God,
by which the rising sun will come to us from heaven
[79]to shine on those living in darkness
and in the shadow of death,
to guide our feet into the path of peace.

These are the circumstances in which the *Benedictus* was first said or sung. Elisabeth (a close relative of the Virgin Mary) had given birth to a son in her old age. Her neighbors and kinsfolk had rejoiced with her over God's goodness. When the boy was eight days old they gathered both to circumcize and to name him. They proposed, according to Jewish custom, to give him his father's name Zacharias (or Zechariah, the Hebrew equivalent), but both his parents were adamant that he should be called John. First Elisabeth said so. Then they made signs to Zacharias, who had evidently become deaf as well as dumb, and he wrote on the wax surface of a writing tablet, "His name is John." To him it was a *fait accompli*. There was no room for debate. The angel had already given him this name before he was conceived (Luke 1:13). Immediately Zacharias's mouth was opened and his tongue loosed, he began to bless God. Either then, or shortly afterwards, he gave utterance to the beautiful song we call the *Benedictus*. If the *Venite* and the *Benedicite* are invitations to praise, addressed respectively to the people of God and to all the *works of the Lord*, the *Benedictus* (like the *Te Deum*) is an actual expression of praise, addressed to God himself. Its theme is thanksgiving for salvation. Indeed, Zacharias's spiritual insight is astonishing. Of course the Virgin Mary had recently stayed with them for three months and no doubt had divulged her secret to them about the baby she was expecting; but Zacharias also received now a direct revelation from God. He knew that the birth of his son would initiate a train of events leading to the salvation of God's people.

So "salvation" is a word echoing through this hymn. It occurs in each of the three paragraphs of the *Benedictus*: *has raised up a horn of salvation for us* (v 69), *salvation from our enemies* (v 71), and *to give his people the knowledge of salvation* (v 77).

Moreover, this *salvation* (which was to be achieved through Jesus Christ) was not an isolated and independent incident. It took place in a prepared context. It was the fulfillment of all Old Testament prediction. So the *Benedictus*, which announces the fulfillment, sees it in the light of the centuries which had anticipated it. The canticle not only refers to such well-known men as Abraham, Israel (Jacob) and David, and the *holy prophets* and Jewish *fathers* in general, but is steeped in the language of the Old Testament. Obvious echoes of Old Testament expressions may be heard in *Praise be to the Lord, the God of Israel* (Psalms 41:13; 72:18; 106:48), *come and has redeemed his people* (Exodus

4:31, Psalm 111:9), *raised up a horn of salvation* (1 Samuel 2:10), *salvation from our enemies* (Psalm 106:10), *to remember his holy covenant* (Leviticus 26:42; Psalms 105:8; 106:45), *the oath he swore to Abraham* (Genesis 22:16, 17; Micah 7:20), *go on before the Lord to prepare the way for him* (Malachi 3:1), *the forgiveness of their sins* (Jeremiah 31:34) and *to shine on those living in darkness* (Isaiah 9:2). It seems probable that the birth narrative, in which the *Benedictus* is embedded, was a very early Aramaic document, which Luke found (or obtained from the Virgin Mary herself, as it is clearly her story), and himself translated into Greek.

The theme of this canticle, then, is the salvation of God in fulfillment of Old Testament promises. It shows very clearly how upon this salvation all prophetic testimony converged. Thus, the word "prophet", or "prophesy", occurs three times. Zacharias is said in Luke 1:67 to be filled with the Holy Ghost and to *prophesy*. We know that he was a priest; he now assumed the role of prophet as well. In verse 3 it is said that God spoke *through his holy prophets long ago*, while in verse 9 Zacharias affirms that his boy John *will be called a prophet of the Most High*. What Zacharias means by prophecy is not so much a prediction of the future, as a direct revelation from God, for essentially a prophet is one through whose mouth God speaks (v 70). He is claiming that the announcement which he is now making, like the announcement which his son John the Baptist will make after him, is nothing other than what the Old Testament prophets have been announcing for centuries. What they said, he is saying; and what he is saying, his son will say after him. The prophets of the past, the present, and the future, all focused their gaze on the same great salvation of God in Christ.

What Zacharias says (vs 68, 69)

Praise be to the Lord, the God of Israel, because he has come and has redeemed his people. He has raised up a horn of salvation for us in the house of his servant David. Zacharias speaks in traditional, prophetic style. His three verbs are aorists—he *has come*, *redeemed*, and *raised up*. He asserts that God has done something which actually he has not yet done, but is about to do. This is the language of the prophets. They sometimes expressed their absolute certainty about some future event by using the so-called "prophetic past tense", What God is about to do, Zacharias indicates in three striking phrases.

First, a visitation: *he has come* (v 68). God is frequently said in the Scriptures to visit this planet. He visited his enslaved people first in Egypt and later in Babylon, in order to deliver them from bondage. He visited Sarah before Isaac was conceived, and Hannah before Samuel was conceived. He is said in Psalm 65 to visit the earth and water it, that it may become fruitful. But his most direct and glorious visitation was in the person of his Son; so that when Jesus once recalled to life the dead son of a widow, the people exclaimed, "God has come to help his people" (Luke 7:16).

Secondly, a redemption: *and has redeemed his people* (v 68). The Scriptures teach that people, whose bodies and minds may be free, are yet slaves of sin, self, greed, and lust, and need to be redeemed. As through his servant Moses God visited and redeemed his people from Egyptian slavery, so through his Son Jesus he came to visit and redeem us from the bondage of sin and death.

Thirdly, *God has raised up a horn of salvation for us in the house of his servant David* (v 69). "Horn" (the natural weapon with which a wild ox attacked and defended itself) was an accepted Old Testament symbol for strength. So "horn of salvation" is rightly translated in the Prayer Book version as *a mighty salvation*. This "horn" was raised up *in the house of... David*. That is, the Savior would belong to the royal line of David. This is not John the Baptist (for his parents were descended from Aaron, not David), but Jesus Christ.

In the next chapter (Luke 2:4) Joseph is described as "being of the house and lineage of David". Mary was also. So the priest-prophet Zacharias, under divine inspiration, announces that in Jesus, the Son of David, God is about to visit, redeem, and save his people in accordance with the promises of the Old Testament.

What the Old Testament prophets said (vs 70-73)

(as he said through his holy prophets of long ago), salvation from our enemies and from the hand of all who hate us—to show mercy to our fathers and to remember his holy covenant, the oath he swore to our father Abraham: (vs 70-73). It would be hard to find a more impressive statement than this, that the age of fulfillment has at last arrived. These verses speak of God's word, his promised mercy, his covenant, and his oath. They assert that what God

spoke to the prophets he has now fulfilled; what he promised to the fathers he has now performed. Again the prophetic past tense is implied. God has kept his words of oath, his covenant and promise, whether they were spoken directly to the early patriarchs or indirectly through the later prophets. God is not a man that he should lie (Numbers 23:19). He stands by his oath, is true to his word, and faithful to his covenant of promise.

This truth is dramatically taught by the Hebrew names of the characters who take part in the story. Zacharias means "God has remembered" (that is, his covenant); Elisabeth means "God is oath" (or "the absolutely faithful one"), while John means "God is, or has been, gracious or merciful".

These divine promises were that we should be saved *from our enemies*, and be delivered out of *the hand of our enemies* (vs 71–74). Both verses speak of a certain salvation, or deliverance, from our enemies, and we may safely assume that these enemies are spiritual, not political. It was not the legions of Rome, or any other foreign foe, from whom men most needed to be saved, but the guilt and power of their sins. This is made clear from verse 10, where the *knowledge of salvation* is explained as *the forgiveness* of *their sins because of the tender mercy of our God*. It is further confirmed by verses 74 and 75, where the result of our deliverance is that *we* should serve God *without fear in holiness and righteousness before him all our days*.

This, then, is how the Old Testament promises of deliverance are to be understood; and this is how they have been fulfilled. God's oath to Abraham was couched in material terms: "your descendants shall possess the gates of their enemies" (Genesis 22:16–18, RSV). Its fulfillment has wonderfully transcended the categories in which it was given. It is a deliverance from sin; a triumph over the world, the flesh and the devil; and a consequent liberty to worship God with holiness, but without fear.

What John the Baptist will say (vs 76–79)

Having uttered a prophecy himself, and spoken of the prophecies of the Old Testament, Zacharias now declares that his son will be a prophet also: *And you, my child, will be called a prophet of the Most High; for you will go on before the Lord to prepare the way for him, to give his people the knowledge of salvation through the forgiveness of their sins, because of the tender mercy of our God by*

*which the rising sun will come to us from heaven to shine on those liv-
ing in darkness and in the shadow of death, to guide our feet into the
path of peace.*

The prophetic function of John will be to act as the forerunner of the Messiah, as already announced by the angel (Luke
1:16, 17). In John the words of the prophecy of Malachi will be
fulfilled: he will go before the face of the Lord, to prepare his
way (3:1). What John will bring to men is not salvation, but the
knowledge of salvation. He is not the Savior, but a witness to the
Savior, of whom he will later say, "Behold the Lamb of God, who
taketh away the sin of the world." The forgiveness of sins John
will promise will be available through God's tender mercy in
sending *the rising sun . . . from heaven* to visit us (v 78).

Jesus was to call himself "the light of the world", as he had
been called in Malachi's prophecy "the sun of righteousness".
Just as the dawn breaks after a long night, so he brought light to
those sitting in darkness and in the shadow of death. Literally,
he made an "epiphany" or "appearance" (to *give light* is
epiphanai), like the sun leaping over the horizon into full view.
Forgiveness (v 77), light, and peace (v 79) are the blessings which
Christ has won for us. This is the meaning of salvation, that
mighty deliverance to which Zacharias, the Old Testament
prophets, and John the Baptist all bore faithful testimony.

Yet when these words were uttered about the salvation of
God, the Savior had not even been born! It is in Luke 1 that
Zacharias describes the greatness of God's salvation; it is not
until Luke 2 that the angels announce the Savior's birth, and the
shepherds go to the manger. Zacharias looked forward with
faith to the coming salvation, although he was so certain of it
that he could speak of it in the prophetic past tense. But we,
more favored than he, can look back to the birth, life, death, and
resurrection of Jesus as accomplished historical facts, through
which our salvation has been achieved.

Luke 1:46-55

The *Magnificat*

The conditions of God's blessing

The circumstances in which the words of the *Magnificat* were first spoken are familiar to all of us. The annunciation that Mary was to be the mother of the Messiah, the Son of God, had just been made to her in Nazareth by the angel Gabriel. The Virgin, overwhelmed by this news, hurried south to the Judean hill country, to share her wonderful secret with her relative Elisabeth, whose son John the Baptist was due to be born in about three months' time. When those two remarkable women met, Elisabeth's unborn child leaped in her womb for joy, as if to salute the Christ whose forerunner he was later to be; and Elisabeth, filled with the Holy Spirit, pronounced Mary blessed among women and called her "the mother of my Lord".

It is hard to imagine the emotion which Mary must have felt on hearing these words. It was wonderful enough that the angel had visited her and told her that her child was to be called "the Son of the Most High". But now Elisabeth and her unborn child

---

[46]And Mary said:
"My soul glorifies the Lord
[47] and my spirit rejoices in God
   my Savior,
[48]for he has been mindful
   of the humble state of his
   servant.
From now on all generations will
   call me blessed,
[49] for the Mighty One has done
   great things for me—
holy is his name.
[50]His mercy extends to those who
   fear him,
   from generation to generation.
[51]He has performed mighty
deeds with his arm;
he has scattered those who are
   proud in their inmost
   thoughts.
[52]He has brought down rulers from
   their thrones
but has lifted up the humble.
[53]He has filled the hungry with
   good things
but has sent the rich away
   empty.
[54]He has helped his servant Israel,
   remembering to be merciful
[55]to Abraham and his descendants
   forever,
even as he said to our fathers."

---

recognized and acknowledged her unique distinction. And Mary, doubly assured of the truth about the child she had conceived, broke forth into this hymn of adoring praise:

> *My soul glorifies the Lord*
> *and my spirit rejoices in God my Savior,*
> *for he has been mindful*
> *of the humble state of his servant.*
> *From now on all generations will call me blessed,*
> *for the Mighty One has done great things for me—*
> *holy is his name.*

These verses are frequently sung as part of the church service. How can we possibly sing these verses? A Hebrew virgin, chosen to be the vehicle of the incarnation of the Son of God, gives inspired expression to her wonderment that she should have been honored in this way. How can we take her words on our lips? Isn't it quite inappropriate—even a little irreverent? But the Christian Church has used the *Magnificat* in the medieval service called Vespers since probably the sixth century A.D., while the Eastern Church includes it among its morning canticles, and it is still popular in the Church of England service of Evening Prayer today.

This is because Christians have recognized that Mary's experience, which in one way was absolutely unique, in another is typical of the experience of every Christian believer. God's amazing grace or mercy, unique in its particular gift to Mary, is yet lavished on us as well. She spoke eloquently of God's sovereign initiative of grace. He had been mindful of the humble state of his servant and done great things for her. He had performed mighty deeds with his arm. He had scattered those who are proud, brought down the rulers, lifted up the humble, filled the hungry, sent the rich away empty. Not unless we think the Virgin Mary is the only person to have experienced these great things that God has done, is it improper or inappropriate for us to sing her song. If we have known anything of God's goodness in doing "great things" for us (v 49), we shall want to rejoice in him and praise him in similar terms.

We can be still more precise in comparing our experience to the Virgin Mary's. Did God give his son to be formed in her body? There is a sense in which Christ may be formed within us. In the same chapter in which the apostle describes God's Son as having been "born of woman", he goes on boldly to write: "My dear children, for whom I am again in the pains of childbirth until Christ is formed in you" (Galatians 4:4, 19; see also 2:20; Ephesians 3:16; Colossians 1:27). It would be difficult to exaggerate the greatness of the Christian's privilege of being indwelt by God the Son, but we can express our wonder and worship in the *Magnificat*.

Mary's awareness that God's dealings with her were not exclusive is clear in the *Magnificat*. After the first four verses she drops the personal pronoun. Having spoken of *God my Savior, who has done great things for me*, she continues, *His mercy extends to those who fear him, from generation to generation*. It is as if she said, "Has God shown mercy to me today? It is because his mercy always extends to those who fear him. Has he regarded my humble state (v 48)? It is because he always lifts up the humble (v 52)."

In order to emphasize that her experience was a particular form of a general principle, Mary quotes liberally from the Old Testament. The *Magnificat* is steeped in Old Testament phraseology. To begin with, it closely resembles the song which Hannah sang after the birth of her son Samuel (1 Samuel 2). Further, it contains at least four direct quotations from Old Testament psalms. *Holy is his name* comes from Psalm 111:9; *His mercy [love] is with those who fear him* from Psalm 103:17; *He fills the hungry with good things* from Psalm 107:9; and *He has remembered his love and his faithfulness to the house of Israel* from Psalm 98:3. Apart from these direct quotations, the whole song breathes the atmosphere, and echoes the language, of the Old Testament. In my Greek New Testament, which prints Old Testament quotations in bold type, out of 102 words which compose the *Magnificat*, 61 are in bold lettering. This means that roughly 60% of the canticle is made up of phrases borrowed from the Old Testament.

This shows how much Mary's mind was saturated in the Old Testament. She had known many of the Old Testament songs by heart since she was a child. She had hidden God's word in her heart. Her memory was richly stored with the Scriptures. So, when filled with the Holy Spirit, she spoke in biblical language.

She saw in her unique privilege an illustration of what God had always been doing and always would do. She was but a poor, common, lowly, God-fearing young girl, eagerly awaiting the kingdom of God, and God had chosen her to give birth to his Son. Was not this just like God? Was not this a striking example of his ways in salvation? He disturbs the settled conventions of men and women and turns their values upside down. The proud are scattered in the foolish imagination of their hearts, while he shows mercy instead to those that fear him. He puts down the rulers from their thrones; it is the humble whom he lifts up. The hungry are filled with good things; the rich he sends empty away. Thus God did to Mary. Thus God has always done. Thus God will also do to us, for these are the principles of his saving activity.

God shows mercy to them that fear him

His mercy extends to those who fear him, from generation to generation. He has performed mighty deeds with his arm; he has scattered those who are proud in their innermost thoughts (vs 50, 51). God's arm scatters the proud; his mercy is over those who fear him. This does not mean those who are afraid of him. There is no commendation here of the timid, the fearful, or the cowardly. The reference is rather to those who reverence and honor God, who stand in awe of his name and tremble at his word.

The bible says much about "the fear of the Lord". We are told in the Psalms, in the book of Job and in Proverbs that "the fear of the LORD is the beginning of wisdom". Part of the indictment of the heathen world is that "there is no fear of God before their eyes." Jesus told us, "Fear him who can destroy both body and soul in hell," referring to his Father in heaven; and the early disciples are described as "walking in the fear of the Lord". There is too much frivolity and irreverence in the world, and even in the Church, today. Men and women have prised open so many locked secrets that there is little left which they regard as sacred. Even in religious circles many people seem to be characterized by a bonhomie which has neither depth nor substance. People have so lost sight of the unfathomable majesty of God, that they have tended to become over-familiar with him. Such people God scatters in the silly imagination of their hearts. His mercy is rather on those who fear him. The Virgin Mary was a simple, devout, God-fearing maiden; we must follow her example if we hope to share her experience.

God exalts the humble

He has brought down rulers from their thrones but has lifted up the humble (v 52). Mary not only feared God; she was also humble. She speaks in her song of her "humble state" (v 48), and gives expression to her amazement that God should have *been mindful* of her. It is not just that she belonged to a lowly social rank, but that she possessed a deep spiritual lowliness and meekness. Therefore God exalted her.

Has it not always been so? God looked in pity on the Israelite slaves, whose lives were being made bitter with hard bondage, and rescued them, while Pharaoh in his pride and pomp was overthrown. He passed over the seven older sons of Jesse, despite all their elegance and experience, and chose his youngest son, David, despite his youth, and called him from the sheepfold to become king of Israel. He caused Daniel, a despised Hebrew youth, to be promoted in the kingdom of Babylon, while Nebuchadnezzar, the arrogant monarch, was driven from his palace, a raving lunatic. Nebuchadnezzar was brought later to understand that "those who walk in pride God is able to humble". This is exactly what Jesus said, "For everyone who exalts himself will be humbled; and he who humbles himself will be exalted." Moreover, this principle was exemplified in his own career. It was because he humbled himself even to death on the cross, that God highly exalted him to his own right hand. The New Testament writers repeat the same truth again and again: "Humble yourselves, therefore, under God's mighty hand, that he may lift you up in due time" (see Daniel 4:37; Luke 18:14; Philippians 2:8, 9; 1 Peter 5:6; James 4:10).

Pride is the greatest hindrance to spiritual progress. Unless we humble ourselves like a little child, we will never enter the kingdom of heaven (Matthew 18:3). If we build thrones and climb up on to them, God will find means to cast us down. Only if we get on our knees with the penitent publican, will he exalt us, both now into acceptance before him and hereafter into his presence in heaven.

God fills the hungry

He has filled the hungry with good things but has sent the rich away empty (v 53). Mary was hungry. Like Zechariah, Elisabeth, Simeon, and Anna, who figure prominently in the infancy narratives, she was waiting for the consolation of Israel and the redemption of Jerusalem. She was not satisfied with things as they were. She had read in the Old Testament what God had promised through the prophets. She knew that one day he would fulfill his promises; that he would redeem his people and establish his kingdom; and that in Abraham's seed all the families of the earth would be blessed. So she waited—eager, expectant, and hungry. In due time God satisfied her hunger; for the Christ was born.

Hunger is still an indispensable condition of spiritual blessing and complacent self-satisfaction its greatest enemy. The *rich*, who are pleased with themselves as they are and have no consciousness of need, God sends away empty. It is the "poor in spirit", who acknowledge their spiritual bankruptcy apart from him, whom he enriches. "Blessed are those who hunger and thirst for righteousness", Jesus said, "for they will be filled." Not unless there is a hunger in our hearts for God and for holiness, is there hope for us today, for it is the hungry alone whom he promises to fill.

If we want to inherit Mary's blessings, we must display Mary's qualities—reverence, humility, and spiritual hunger.

In conclusion, the Virgin Mary turns from herself (vs 46–49), and all who like her fear God and are humble and hungry (vs 50–53), to the nation of Israel (vs 54–55). She recognizes that in sending his Son the Messiah, God had not only done a great thing for her personally and exalted the humble, but had also *helped his servant Israel*. After the long years of the nation's expectancy God had come to their aid, in remembrance of his mercy, and in fulfilment of the eternal covenant which he had made with Abraham and his posterity.

Luke 2:29-32

The *Nunc Dimittis*

Christ brings light and peace

There is something peculiarly touching about the *Nunc Dimittis*, which has been a favorite to be sung in Christian worship from very early days. It is found already at end of the fourth century, and according to tradition Pope Gregory the Great introduced it into the service of Compline at the end of the fifth century. Here Archbishop Thomas Cranmer found it, and fittingly inserted it in his Episcopalian Prayer Book to be sung during the service of Evening Prayer.

Simeon was an elderly inhabitant of Jerusalem. We do not know who he was; but we are told that he was "righteous and devout" (Luke 2:25), or (as we might say) "a good man, and religious". He was righteous in his conduct and conscientious in his religious duties. At the end of the same verse it is written that "the Holy Spirit was upon him". Some time before the Holy Spirit was poured out on the day of Pentecost, Simeon had an unusual experience of his presence and power.

Another mark of Simeon's character was his complete surrender to God. He began his song by addressing God as *Lord*. This is not the common Greek word *kurios*, but *despotes*, meaning "Sovereign Lord". It occurs in the New Testament only three times as a title of God, and only twice of Jesus Christ. It is the word used of the slave-owner who had absolute possession of his slaves.

Something special is then added. Simeon is said to have been "waiting for the consolation of Israel". That is, he was wait-

²⁹Sovereign Lord, as you have promised,
    you now dismiss your servant
    in peace.
³⁰For my eyes have seen your salvation,
	³¹ which you have prepared in the sight of all people,
	³²a light for revelation to the Gentiles
	    and for glory to your people Israel.

ing expectantly for the coming of the Messiah. The rabbis used sometimes to call the Messiah the "Comforter", because they knew that only in his days would the great prophecy of Isaiah 40:1-2 be fulfilled:

> Comfort, comfort my people,
> says your God.
> Speak tenderly to Jerusalem...

Moreover, God had somehow revealed to Simeon that his expectation would be fulfilled during his lifetime. The Messiah was about to be born, and Simeon would "see the Lord's Christ", that is the Lord's anointed or Messianic king, before he died. Perhaps, then, we can visualize this old man, no doubt bearded, venerable, and with his faculties failing, frequenting the Temple at Jerusalem, and waiting day after day for the fulfillment of God's promise to him. One day Joseph and Mary brought the infant Jesus into the Temple, to perform certain ceremonial rites which were required by the law of Moses. When Simeon saw this holy baby, he knew that his time of waiting was over. He took the child in his arms, blessed God, and said: *Sovereign Lord, as you have promised, you now dismiss your servant in peace. For my eyes have seen your salvation.*

Already Joseph had been told that the baby to be born should be called Jesus, because he was going to save his people from their sins. Already the angel had announced to the shepherds in the fields near Bethlehem, "Today in the town of David a Savior has been born to you" (Matthew 1:21; Luke 2:11). Now simeon takes up the glorious theme. Mary's baby is the salvation of God. Through him God is going to work out the salvation of humankind. Through him men and women will be delivered from their sins and set free from bondage.

Simeon's song is devoted to expounding the blessings of this salvation. We consider them in the opposite order to that in which he mentions them.

Glory to Israel

...glory to your people, Israel (v 32). Simeon, who had been waiting for the consolation of Israel, recognized in Jesus the one who would bring to Israel not only consolation but glory. And what glory Jesus has brought to Israel! He himself later said that "sal-

vation is of the Jews". That is to say, it is from the Jewish nation that God's salvation has come to us. It is to the Jews that we owe our Savior. He was born, according to the flesh, of the seed of David.

Anti-Semitic prejudice is particularly unacceptable in a Christian. Although we are grieved that many Jews today do not recognize in Jesus their Savior and their Messiah, we can never forget that it is to them as a people that we owe him.

Previously God had given Israel the patriarchs, the covenants of promise, the law, and the prophets. But now, as their crowning glory, he gave them his only begotten Son, to be born of a Hebrew peasant girl. So Jesus and his salvation are the *glory to* God's *people, Israel.*

Light to the nations

My eyes have seen your salvation, which you have prepared in the sight of all people, a light for revelation to the Gentiles... (vs 30–32). With a remarkable flash of prophetic vision this Jew, resident in the Jewish capital, realized that Christ's light, besides casting a luster upon Israel, was to illumine the darkness of the heathen nations. So he quoted with reference to the child in his arms the great prophecy of one of Isaiah's Servant songs: "I will also make you a light for the Gentiles, that you may bring my salvation to the ends of the earth" (Isaiah 49:6). Ignorance, superstition, idolatry, fear, sin—these are the dark and somber clouds which the light of Christ was to dispel. Such was his own claim in years to come: "I am the light of the world. Whoever follows me will never walk in darkness, but will have the light of life" (John 8:12).

Jesus is the light of the *world*. We cannot therefore keep him to ourselves. We dare not attempt to monopolize him. Christianity is inescapably and unashamedly a missionary faith. We are committed to spread it. We cannot rest until every inhabitant of the globe has heard of him and God's salvation in him. In this work every Christian has a part to play, whether by witness, prayers, or gifts.

Peace to the individual

Sovereign Lord, as you have promised, you now dismiss your servant in peace. For my eyes have seen your salvation (vs 29, 30). Simeon had been told that he would not die until he had seen the Lord's Christ. But now that he had seen Jesus, he was quite ready to die, for he recognized him as God's salvation. Moreover, he had made this salvation his own by faith, taking the babe in his own arms. He seems even to have regarded this life as a kind of bondage, since the Greek verb should literally be translated: "Lord... you now *release* your slave.

This attitude to death is not shared by many today. Most people are afraid to die. How can we have Simeon's quiet assurance in the face of death? Only by sharing Simeon's faith, seeing in Jesus the salvation of God, and receiving him for ourselves. Simeon evidently anticipated that Jesus was going to suffer (Luke 2:34, 35). We know that it was for our sins that he suffered and died, bearing them in his own sacred person. Through his death there is a full and free forgiveness for every one who puts his or her trust in him. Simeon took him up in his arms; we must embrace him by faith. Besides, he rose again from death. He broke out of his prison sepulcher. He shattered the bars of death. He vanquished this ancient enemy of humanity.

If Jesus Christ, crucified and risen, is our Savior, we have peace with God and therefore have no reason to be afraid of death. We can say with aged Simeon: *Lord, you now dismiss your servant in peace.*